er Books of Related Interest:

sing Viewpoints Series

otics

Drug Abuse

sue Series

nericans Overmedicated?

ent Controversies Series

Legalization

Care

al Ethics

al Marijuana

ninsured

al Viewpoints Series

al Ethics

ducing Issues with Opposing
points Series

es

s That Concern You Series

OPPOSING VIEWPOINTS® SERIES

The
Pharmaceutical In

"Congress shall make
no law . . . abridging
the freedom of speech,
or of the press."

First Amendment to the US Constitution

The basic foundation of our democracy is the First Amendment guarantee of freedom of expression. The Opposing Viewpoints Series is dedicated to the concept of this basic freedom and the idea that it is more important to practice it than to enshrine it.

OPPOSING VIEWPOINTS® SERIES

The Pharmaceutical Industry

Roman Espejo, Book Editor

GREENHAVEN PRESS
A part of Gale, Cengage Learning

GALE
CENGAGE Learning·

Detroit • New York • San Francisco • New Haven, Conn • Waterville, Maine • London

Elizabeth Des Chenes, *Managing Editor*

© 2012 Greenhaven Press, a part of Gale, Cengage Learning.

Gale and Greenhaven Press are registered trademarks used herein under license.

For more information, contact:
Greenhaven Press
27500 Drake Rd.
Farmington Hills, MI 48331-3535
Or you can visit our Internet site at gale.cengage.com

LIBRARY OF CONGRESS CATALOGING-IN-PUBLICATION DATA

The pharmaceutical industry / Roman Espejo, book editor.
    p. cm. -- (Opposing viewpoints)
Summary: "The Pharmaceutical Industry: Is Pharmaceutical Research Safe and Unbiased?; Are Prescription Drugs Appropriately Regulated?; Are Pharmaceutical Marketing Practices Ethical?; Is the Cost of Prescription Drugs in America Appropriate?"-- Provided by publisher.
    Includes bibliographical references and index.
    ISBN 978-0-7377-5753-8 (hardback) -- ISBN 978-0-7377-5754-5 (pbk.)
    1. Drugs--Research--Popular works. 2. Pharmaceutical industry--Popular works. I. Espejo, Roman, 1977-
    RM301.15.P477 2011
    338.4'76151--dc23

                                                                    2011023749

Printed in Mexico
2 3 4 5 6 7 15 14 13 12

Contents

Why Consider Opposing Viewpoints?

"The only way in which a human being can make some approach to knowing the whole of a subject is by hearing what can be said about it by persons of every variety of opinion and studying all modes in which it can be looked at by every character of mind. No wise man ever acquired his wisdom in any mode but this."

John Stuart Mill

In our media-intensive culture it is not difficult to find differing opinions. Thousands of newspapers and magazines and dozens of radio and television talk shows resound with differing points of view. The difficulty lies in deciding which opinion to agree with and which "experts" seem the most credible. The more inundated we become with differing opinions and claims, the more essential it is to hone critical reading and thinking skills to evaluate these ideas. Opposing Viewpoints books address this problem directly by presenting stimulating debates that can be used to enhance and teach these skills. The varied opinions contained in each book examine many different aspects of a single issue. While examining these conveniently edited opposing views, readers can develop critical thinking skills such as the ability to compare and contrast authors' credibility, facts, argumentation styles, use of persuasive techniques, and other stylistic tools. In short, the Opposing Viewpoints Series is an ideal way to attain the higher-level thinking and reading skills so essential in a culture of diverse and contradictory opinions.

In addition to providing a tool for critical thinking, Opposing Viewpoints books challenge readers to question their own strongly held opinions and assumptions. Most people form their opinions on the basis of upbringing, peer pressure, and personal, cultural, or professional bias. By reading carefully balanced opposing views, readers must directly confront new ideas as well as the opinions of those with whom they disagree. This is not to simplistically argue that everyone who reads opposing views will—or should—change his or her opinion. Instead, the series enhances readers' understanding of their own views by encouraging confrontation with opposing ideas. Careful examination of others' views can lead to the readers' understanding of the logical inconsistencies in their own opinions, perspective on why they hold an opinion, and the consideration of the possibility that their opinion requires further evaluation.

Evaluating Other Opinions

To ensure that this type of examination occurs, Opposing Viewpoints books present all types of opinions. Prominent spokespeople on different sides of each issue as well as well-known professionals from many disciplines challenge the reader. An additional goal of the series is to provide a forum for other, less known, or even unpopular viewpoints. The opinion of an ordinary person who has had to make the decision to cut off life support from a terminally ill relative, for example, may be just as valuable and provide just as much insight as a medical ethicist's professional opinion. The editors have two additional purposes in including these less known views. One, the editors encourage readers to respect others' opinions—even when not enhanced by professional credibility. It is only by reading or listening to and objectively evaluating others' ideas that one can determine whether they are worthy of consideration. Two, the inclusion of such viewpoints encourages the important critical thinking skill of objectively evaluating an author's credentials and bias. This evaluation will illuminate an author's reasons for taking a particular stance on an issue and will aid in readers' evaluation of the author's ideas.

It is our hope that these books will give readers a deeper understanding of the issues debated and an appreciation of the complexity of even seemingly simple issues when good and honest people disagree. This awareness is particularly important in a democratic society such as ours in which people enter into public debate to determine the common good. Those with whom one disagrees should not be regarded as enemies but rather as people whose views deserve careful examination and may shed light on one's own.

Thomas Jefferson once said that "difference of opinion leads to inquiry, and inquiry to truth." Jefferson, a broadly educated man, argued that "if a nation expects to be ignorant and free . . . it expects what never was and never will be." As individuals and as a nation, it is imperative that we consider the opinions of others and examine them with skill and discernment. The Opposing Viewpoints Series is intended to help readers achieve this goal.

David L. Bender and Bruno Leone,
Founders

Introduction

"Internet reimportation has become a 'virtual lifeline' for millions of Americans."

—Rx Rights National
Coalition for Drug Importation

"Politicians need to be conscious of the longer-term, far-reaching harmful effects that their well-intentioned but misguided policies on drug importation may have on their local citizens, companies, and economy."

—Douglas Giuffre,
Beacon Hill Institute economist

When American-made medicines are purchased abroad for a lower price and brought back into the United States, it is known as drug reimportation. Under Section 804 of the federal Food, Drug, and Cosmetic Act, Americans seeking lower prices for prescription drugs can reimport up to a ninety-day supply from Canada for personal use. The Canadian government controls how much manufacturers can charge for prescription drugs and places caps on prices. Also, provincial governments negotiate prices with manufacturers on the basis of the drugs' medical efficacy and enforce their own policies on markups. And pharmaceutical companies in Canada cannot advertise directly to consumers, reducing prices even further. Moreover, generics there are released five years earlier than in the United States and must cost at least 25 percent less than the brand-name drug.

Despite her doubts, Linda Covella, a writer living in Santa Cruz, California, decided to purchase her prescription from a

Canadian online pharmacy after her insurance deductible was raised, requiring her to pay more than $400 of the total $700. "The process was easy, the Canadian pharmacist and pharmacy staff helpful, and I'm alive and well," Covella says. "In other words, the pills were completely safe and trustworthy. And cost $150 instead of $400," she smiles, while noting that such savings ring in virtually across the board. "You'll find amazing differences between Canadian drug prices and those in the US for most prescription medications,"[1] she claims.

Before Americans could log onto one of the dozens of licensed Canadian online pharmacies to fill their prescriptions, they crossed its border on buses for cheaper medications. A longtime supporter of drug importation, Lee Graczyk arranged these trips as the senior public policy director of the Minnesota Senior Federation. To fund them, former US senator from Minnesota Mark Dayton donated his senator's salary to the Minnesota Senior Federation for his six-year term. In addition, Graczyk investigated more than twenty Canadian pharmacists for the program, choosing those with the highest standards. Now, with more than twenty-two hundred members, the program operates under Mature Voices Minnesota. "Drug reimportation is critical to lowering prices," maintains Congressman Ron Paul, who was a physician for almost four decades before becoming a Texas representative in Congress. "Reimportation allows American consumers, particularly seniors, to benefit from worldwide price competition,"[2] he adds. Additionally, a Boston University study reports that the influx of cheaper foreign pills would turn individuals who can only afford to take medication if they split pills, skip doses, or do not fill their prescriptions at all into full-fledged customers, which would be a boon to drug companies.

Critics, however, claim that reimporting pharmaceuticals would set back innovations in the field. "If the United States imports price controls from Canada, drug costs may drop, but so will drug research and development," contends James K. Glassman, journalist and executive director of the George W. Bush Institute. "Canadians and Europeans are 'free riders.' They benefit from research that is paid for by American consumers,"[3] Glassman says. For instance, he cites a study showing that if price controls existed between 1981 and 2002 in the United States, there would be up to 365 fewer drugs available on the market. Other critics also counter the position that drug reimportation is advantageous to Americans. "Even if importation were to lead to lower-priced drugs," speculates Nina Owcharenko, a research director at the Heritage Foundation, a Washington, DC, think tank. "The real winners might not be consumers; wholesalers could buy drugs at lower prices but would not necessarily pass those savings on to their customers," [4] she adds. The safety of imported drugs—even reimported ones—is questioned, too. "Studies have shown that a significant percentage of drugs thought to be American-made and reimported are actually counterfeit, ineffective, or even toxic," contends Gilbert Ross, medical director of the American Council on Science and Health. "In one sting in 2003, for example, FDA and Customs officials found that 88 percent of the imported drug packages they inspected did not meet FDA safety standards,"[5] he reports.

The unrivaled cost of prescription drugs in the United States continues to be a polarizing issue, from the enormous investments in research and development to the cutting-edge treatments of tomorrow being used today. *Opposing Viewpoints: The Pharmaceutical Industry* examines these and other topics in the following chapters: Is Pharmaceutical Research Safe and Unbiased? Does the FDA Effectively Regulate Prescription Drugs? Are Pharmaceutical Marketing Practices Adequately Regulated? and Is the Cost of Prescription Drugs in America Appropriate? The authors in this volume examine the modern-day drug industry as it surpasses two centuries of discovery and controversy.

Notes

1. Quoted in "The Canadian Connection for Affordable Drugs," SantaCruzPatch, April 11, 2011. http://santacruz .patch.com/articles/the-canadian-connection.

2. Ron Paul, "Free Trade in Pharmceuticals," LewRockwell.com, June 26, 2003. www.lewrockwell.com/paul/paul105.html.

3. James K. Glassman, "Drugs from Abroad—California or Bust?," SFGate.com, June 10, 2004. http://articles.sfgate.com/ 2004-06-10/opinion/17429256_1_price-controls-new-medi cines-new-drugs/2.

4. Nina Owcharenko, "Debunking the Myths of Drug Importation," Heritage Foundation WebMemo #542, July 20, 2004. www.heritage.org/research/reports/2004/07/debunk ing-the-myths-of-drug-importation.

5. Gilbert Ross, "Why Drug 'Reimportation' Won't Die," *Wall Street Journal*, January 7, 2010. http://online.wsj.com/article/ SB10001424052748704842604574642184130409874.html.

CHAPTER 1

Is Pharmaceutical Research Safe and Unbiased?

Chapter Preface

In 2005, eight out of ten prescription drugs on the US market were withdrawn due to adverse effects on women's health. "This represents an enormous waste of research money as a consequence of neglecting gender research," argues Anita Holdcroft, a researcher and deputy chair of the British Medical Association Medical Academic Staff Committee. "The evidence basis of medicine may be fundamentally flawed because there is an ongoing failure of research tools to include sex differences in study design and analysis," she adds. Furthermore, she asserts that research funding for coronary heart disease is biased toward men despite the higher rates of morbidity and mortality for women who are at risk. "The lack of funding for women's disease in effect maintains women's lower economic status," Holdcroft contends. "It can also hinder research into gender medicine where significant advances in the diagnosis and management of coronary artery disease have built up from small differences into major gender medicine issues,"[1] she notes.

Nonetheless, other commentators disagree that gender biases exist in drug research. Columnist Cathy Young and psychiatrist Sally Satel hold the opinion that it is logical for some coronary heart disease studies to exclude female subjects. "A study of the effectiveness of heart attack prevention requires a group which would normally have a relatively high rate of heart attacks," they claim. "Before 65, heart attacks kill men three times as often as women; between 65 and 74, the ratio is two to one." In fact, Young and Satel contend that the power of women in health care and medicine has markedly improved: "Women have become more assertive and better-informed patients. And there are unprecedented numbers of

1. Anita Holdcroft, "Gender Bias in Research: How Does It Affect Evidence Based Medicine?," *Journal of the Royal Society of Medicine*, January 2007.

women in the medical profession, as practicing physicians and as researchers."[2] In the following chapter, the authors debate the levels of bias and safety in pharmaceutical trials.

2. Cathy Young and Sally Satel, "The Myth of Gender Bias in Medicine," *Mensight Magazine* (revised February 10, 2005). http://mensightmagazine.com/Library/genmed bias.htm.

| "Clinical trials are crucial forces in the war against cancer."

Pharmaceutical Clinical Trials Save Lives

Leslie Brody

Leslie Brody is a staff writer for the Record, *a daily newspaper serving Bergen County, New Jersey. In the following viewpoint, Brody contends that clinical trials are crucial in the development of cancer-fighting drugs. While facing unknown risks and severe side effects, trial volunteers gain access to cutting-edge treatment when standard therapies have failed, Brody maintains. In addition, the author claims that clinical trials comply with rigorous federal regulations and are overseen by an independent review board. The difficulty of recruiting volunteers, however, is a barrier to filling trials and bringing experimental drugs and technologies into use, Brody contends.*

As you read, consider the following questions:

1. What percentage of eligible adult cancer patients sign up for clinical trials, according to the author?

2. What happens when cancer patients consider a clinical trial as a last resort, in Brody's view?

3. As stated by Brody, what happens in Phase III trials?

As soon as Carolyn Chasalow learned she had pancreatic cancer, she joined a research study of a new chemotherapy regimen. The lethal disease had already hit her liver, so she figured she had little to lose.

Her decision more than a year and a half ago paid off. The tumors have shrunk significantly, she feels fine most days and even teaches water aerobics at 73. She hopes the drugs will keep working for years. "I'm one of the lucky ones," she says with quiet grace.

Carolyn and other courageous volunteers in clinical trials are crucial forces in the war against cancer. To the enormous frustration of many scientists, however, only a tiny fraction of patients sign up. Only 3 percent to 5 percent of eligible adult cancer patients take part in trials, according to the Coalition of Cancer Cooperative Groups, which advocates for higher enrollment.

Thanks to the great pace of discoveries in the lab, there's a huge demand for patients willing to test experimental approaches. Doctors say the difficulty filling trials is one of the top barriers—along with insufficient research dollars—to improving cancer care. More than 5,000 cancer clinical trials are under way nationwide. Recruiting enough patients to fill one often takes years.

"This is a very sophisticated community but there's still a very small percentage who are comfortable going into clinical trials," says Dr. Richard Michaelson, chief medical officer for oncology at St. Barnabas Medical Center in Livingston [New Jersey]. "The technology in the lab is amazing these days . . . but unless treatments are tested in clinical trials, they'll never be incorporated into use."

Patients in the early steps of testing, known as Phase I and II, often face unknown risks but can also be the very first to benefit from cutting-edge medicine.

Many patients, however, are leery of feeling like "guinea pigs." So it is for my 57-year-old husband, Elliot, who has been fighting pancreatic cancer for more than a year and a half. Fortunately, he feels strong and seems stable as he plugs away with standard chemotherapies, getting intravenous infusions every two weeks. It's tiring on top of work, but manageable.

Considering the dismal statistics for pancreatic cancer (only 5 percent of patients survive five years) we can't help wondering if there might be some more promising treatment out there. A little magic would be nice. At times we have gingerly discussed trying something experimental.

When we heard about Carolyn's success recently, our interest was certainly piqued. Her doctor at Morristown Memorial Hospital, Stephen Schreibman, says she's had one of the best responses so far in a Phase II study of the drug combination called GTX. Its investigators are so optimistic about its power they hope it will become accepted as standard.

Other doctors, however, have found more modest results for GTX and say it has harsh side effects in some patients.

My husband's oncologist, Dr. David P. Kelsen at Memorial Sloan-Kettering Cancer Center, is an ardent advocate for joining research studies when appropriate, but says this is not the time for us to try one. As long as Elliot's current treatment is effective, he says, "it would be strange to switch to something unproven."

At each crossroad, however, Kelsen has raised the idea of a trial—when Elliot was first diagnosed and when his first line of chemotherapy stopped working a year ago. At some point this second set of drugs is likely to fail as well, and experi-

Clinical Trials Provide Sense of Benefit

While most new drug therapies are tested individually, they are almost always tested against a control regimen of all previously used therapy. Thus, the clinical trial results give us a sense of how much incremental benefit a new therapy brings to the usual therapeutic package that was available before. On average, the incremental improvement in important patient outcomes, like survival, has traditionally been about 20 percent for most drugs accepted as being efficacious in clinical trial settings. This means that a proven efficacious drug, compared to its absence, would offer about a 20 percent improvement in an outcome like survival, over some time frame—such as a week, a year or even multiple years—during which patients were studied in the trial.

Terrence J. Montague, Patients First: Closing the Health Care Gap in Canada, *2004.*

mental options will come up again. "Whenever a treatment decision needs to be made," Kelsen says, "clinical trials should be considered."

Researching this story is my way of getting ready for that scary day. We will need to be open-minded.

It Is Wise to Think Ahead

Many scientists wish families wouldn't think of clinical trials as a last resort. Unfortunately, by the time some people are willing to join one, they can't; they're too sick or have taken too many other medicines to be eligible. Drug trials have strict criteria for admission.

That's why doctors at the Cancer Institute of New Jersey in New Brunswick encourage patients to consider clinical trials when they're first diagnosed and throughout their illness, says Dr. Susan Goodin, director of pharmaceutical sciences. In many cases, she says, it can be useful to join a trial first, then fall back on standard therapy if need be. She calls the battle against cancer a "chess match"; it's wise to plan several moves ahead.

"Every time patients make a decision, they could very well be limiting their ability to get the next treatment," she says.

Joining a study has compelling advantages. Sometimes it's the only way to get state-of-the-art drugs. You can take pride in helping others. You can drop out any time. Cancer treatment trials almost never use placebos, so you don't have to worry you might get a mere sugar pill.

Phase III trials assign patients to two groups randomly, to compare a new treatment against the current standard. If you're in the investigational group, you'll get the new therapy being tested. If you're in the control group, you'll get the most widely accepted treatment. (In some cases, a study compares standard care plus a new treatment to standard care plus a placebo. If so, you will be told the study has a placebo.)

The disadvantages of a trial, on the other hand, can be daunting. You might suffer severe, unknown side effects. Blood tests and scans might be more frequent. You might have to travel to a major medical center.

Some skeptics charge that a few doctors running trials might be more motivated by prestige or profit than the well-being of patients. To prevent unscrupulous behavior, clinical trials must comply with rigorous federal rules and auditing. Every trial is overseen by an Institutional Review Board, an independent group of doctors, statisticians and community advocates charged with ensuring the study is ethical. Doctors are supposed to disclose any financial stake in its outcome.

Grasping at Straws

Kathleen van Beveren, a 55-year-old from Little Falls, feels too desperate to shy away. Two standard therapies failed to control her rare sarcoma, so she recently joined a Phase I study at the Cancer Institute of New Jersey.

On her kitchen wall hangs a detailed calendar telling her when to come in for infusions and tests and when to eat to minimize nausea. "It's all grasping at straws," she says, "but I feel they've given me some hope."

Sometimes a decision to join a trial boils down to the doctor's pitch or the patient's personality.

Ted, a 53-year-old in New Providence, says that as an engineer, he appreciates the value and difficulty of collecting good data. After colon cancer surgery in August, his doctors at Saint Barnabas offered him a Phase III trial to see if a new drug combination would prevent recurrence.

"My attitude was, why not give it a shot?" Ted says. "At minimum it would provide some data for folks, and maybe it would help. . . . Some people have the notion there's a magic elixir in the trial—but if they knew that, they'd give it to everyone."

He pored over data to make his choice.

If he skipped chemo, he had a 40 percent chance of living at least five years. If he took the standard chemo, he had a 65 percent chance. If he got the trial combination, he faced several risks, but he might live longer.

"We talk about these things as analytically as we can, and play the odds," says Ted, who ended up in the trial group. "I'm bullish on its success."

Many patients don't enter trials simply because they don't know about the option.

Oncologists say many doctors don't recruit for studies because of the paperwork burdens of participating.

Michaelson at Saint Barnabas suggests a more emotional point; he says some doctors might resist spelling out the bad news that could spur patients to brave experimental agents. "We may be hesitant to let people know how difficult their situations might be," he says.

My husband would certainly rather pore over baseball statistics than the ugly mortality rates of various cancer treatments, but at some point we might have no choice.

New drug trials are "marketing in hope," as Elliot puts it. "You want to make sure that hope is reasonable."

VIEWPOINT

> *"The danger lies . . . in a system of clini-*
> *cal research that has been thoroughly*
> *co-opted by market forces, so that many*
> *studies have become little more than*
> *covert instruments for promoting*
> *drugs."*

Pharmaceutical Clinical Trials Imperil Lives

Carl Elliot

In the following viewpoint, Carl Elliot argues that pharmaceuti-
cal clinical trials are designed to promote drugs and generate
profits, thus endangering lives. He recounts the death of Dan
Weiss, a psychiatric patient who killed himself during an anti-
psychotic drug study at the University of Minnesota. According
to Elliot, Weiss was coerced to participate despite his mother's
opposition and repeated warnings for his safety. An investigation
of the medical records and trial, the author alleges, reveals fi-
nancial incentives for Weiss's physician and the university and
manipulated research findings of little scientific value. Elliott is a
bioethics professor at the University of Minnesota and author of
White Coat, Black Hat: Adventures on the Dark Side of Medicine.

As you read, consider the following questions:

1. What were the risks to the patients in the CAFE study, as described by Elliot?

2. As stated by the author, what financial arrangements did the University of Minnesota have to conduct the CAFE study?

3. How did the CAFE study measure the effectiveness of an antipsychotic medication, as claimed by Elliot?

It's not easy to work up a good feeling about the institution that destroyed your life, which may be why Mary Weiss initially seemed a little reluctant to meet me. "You can understand my hesitation to look other than with suspicion at anyone associated with the University of Minnesota," Mary wrote to me in an email. In 2003, Mary's 26-year-old son, Dan, was enrolled against her wishes in a psychiatric drug study at the University of Minnesota, where I teach medical ethics. Less than six months later, Dan was dead. I'd learned about his death from a deeply unsettling newspaper series by *St. Paul Pioneer Press* reporters Jeremy Olson and Paul Tosto that suggested he was coerced into a pharmaceutical-industry study from which the university stood to profit, but which provided him with inadequate care. Over the next few months, I talked to several university colleagues and administrators, trying to learn what had happened. Many of them dismissed the story as slanted and incomplete. Yet the more I examined the medical and court records, the more I became convinced that the problem was worse than the *Pioneer Press* had reported. The danger lies not just in the particular circumstances that led to Dan's death, but in a system of clinical research that has been thoroughly co-opted by market forces, so that many studies have become little more than covert instruments for promoting drugs. The study in which Dan died starkly illustrates the hazards of market-driven research and the inadequacy of our current oversight system to detect them. . . .

When Mary went out to Los Angeles for a visit in the summer of 2003, it was clear Dan had changed. He'd adopted a new last name, Markingson. His behavior was bizarre. "He said, 'You haven't told me when the event is going to be,'" Mary said. She had no idea what he was talking about. The next day, he took her to his apartment. He'd encircled his bed with wooden posts, salt, candles, and money, which he said would protect him from evil spirits. He showed her a spot on the carpet that he said the aliens had burned.

I asked Mary how she'd reacted to all of this. "I panicked. I called 911," she replied. But when the police arrived, Dan was able to convince them she had overreacted. "He said, 'Oh, my mother just drove from Minnesota and she's very tired,'" she recalled. Worried that Dan was seriously ill, she tried to convince him to return to St. Paul. He visited her in August, returned briefly to California, and then came back to St. Paul in October.

Dan grew convinced that the illuminati [an alleged secret society masterminding world events] were orchestrating an event in Duluth, Minnesota—a "storm" in which he would be called upon to murder people, including Mary. . . .

On November 12, Dan said he would kill Mary if called upon to do so. She called the police. Dan was taken to Regions Hospital in St. Paul. But the hospital had no psychiatric beds available, so after a few hours Dan was transferred to Fairview University Medical Center, a teaching hospital for the University of Minnesota Academic Health Center. He was treated by Dr. Stephen C. Olson, an associate professor in the university's psychiatry department, who prescribed Dan Risperdal (risperidone), an antipsychotic drug often prescribed for patients with schizophrenia or bipolar disorder. (In Minnesota, doctors are allowed to give antipsychotic drugs to mentally incompetent patients without their consent for up to 14 days, but only to prevent serious, immediate physical harm to the patient or others.) Olson believed Dan was psychotic and dangerous, and lacked the ability to make decisions regarding his treatment; on November 14 he signed a document that recommended Dan be committed involuntarily to a state mental institution, noting that he "lacks the capacity to make decisions regarding such treatment." Three days later, a clinical psychologist also recommended involuntary commitment, reiterating that Dan had threatened to slit his mother's throat.

In Minnesota, patients who have been involuntarily committed are given another option: a "stay of commitment." Patients can avoid being confined to a mental institution as long as they agree to comply with the treatment program laid out by their psychiatrist. On November 20, Olson asked for a stay of commitment. The court granted the stay for six months, stipulating that Dan had to follow the recommendations of his treatment team. Olson, however, did not simply recommend standard medical treatment. Instead, he proposed that Dan take part in an industry-funded study of antipsychotic drugs. The university's study coordinator, Jean Kenney, had Dan sign a consent form when Mary wasn't present, and on November 21, he was enrolled in the study.

On the Surface

On the surface, the study appeared benign. Its purpose was to compare the effectiveness of three "atypical" antipsychotic drugs, each of which had already been approved by the FDA [Food and Drug Administration]: Seroquel (quetiapine), Zyprexa (olanzapine), and Risperdal (risperidone.) The study was designed and funded by AstraZeneca, the manufacturer of Seroquel, and it called for 400 subjects experiencing their first psychotic episode to take one of the three drugs for a year. AstraZeneca called it the "CAFE" study, which stood for "Comparison of Atypicals in First Episode." The management of the CAFE study had been outsourced to Quintiles, a contract research organization [CRO], which was conducting it at 26 different sites, including the University of Minnesota.

Yet the CAFE study was not without risks. It barred subjects from being taken off their assigned drug; it didn't allow them to be switched to another drug if their assigned drug was not working; and it restricted the number of additional drugs subjects could be given to manage side effects and symptoms such as depression, anxiety, or agitation. Like many clinical trials, the study was also randomized and double-blinded: Subjects were assigned a drug randomly by a computer, and neither the subjects nor the researchers knew which drug it was. These restrictions meant that subjects in the CAFE study had fewer therapeutic options than they would have had outside the study.

In fact, the CAFE study also contained a serious oversight that, if corrected, would have prevented patients like Dan from being enrolled. Like other patients with schizophrenia, patients experiencing their first psychotic episode are at higher risk of killing themselves or other people. For this reason, most studies of antipsychotic drugs specifically bar researchers from recruiting patients at risk of violence or suicide, for fear that they might kill themselves or someone else during the study. Conveniently, however, the CAFE study only prohibited patients at risk of suicide, not homicide. This meant that Dan—who had threatened to slit his mother's throat, but had not threatened to harm himself—was a legitimate target for recruitment.

When Mary found out that Dan had been recruited into the CAFE study, she was stunned. "I do not want him in a clinical study," she told Olson. Just a few days earlier, Olson indicated in a petition to the court that Dan was both dangerous and mentally incapable of consenting to antipsychotic medication. How could he now be capable of consenting to a research study with the very same antipsychotics—especially when the alternative was commitment to a state mental institution?

After Dan was enrolled, he stayed at Fairview for about two more weeks. By that point, Olson thought Dan's symptoms were under control, but Mary was still very worried by his erratic behavior. She recalls meeting with the doctor: "Olson came in and sat down and opened his file and said, 'Oh, Dan is doing so well.' And I said, 'No, Dr. Olson, Dan is not doing well.' I think he was taken aback." Even so, on December 8, 2003, Dan was transferred to Theo House, a halfway house in St. Paul. He was required to sign an agreement confirming that he understood he could be involuntarily committed if he didn't continue taking his medication and keeping his CAFE study appointments.

At the halfway house, Dan often stayed in his room for days. On March 26, 2004 nearly four months after his discharge from Fairview, his thoughts were still "delusional and grandiose," according to a social worker's note. An occupational-therapy report from April 30 detailed Dan's condition: "Personal appearance disheveled. Isolated and withdrawn. Poor insight and self-awareness." Entries in a personal journal that Dan kept during this period don't show any obvious changes, suggesting that he was improving little, if at all. Mary felt he was becoming angrier. "He was so tense, with this ready-to-explode quality."

Olson saw things differently. "I disagree that he had significant deterioration," he testified in a 2007 deposition. However, it's unclear whether Olson actually saw Dan enough to make an informed judgment about his condition. Records suggest most of Dan's care was managed by social workers. In his deposition, Olson said he saw Dan approximately six times from the date he was admitted in November until he committed suicide in May. Whatever the doctor thought, his actions don't suggest that he felt Dan was improving. In late April 2004, as Dan's stay of commitment was about to expire, Olson recommended extending it for another six months—the duration of the CAFE study. He noted that Dan still had "little insight into his mental disorder" and might "place himself at risk of harm if he were to terminate his treatment."

Communicating Her Alarm

Mary tried to get Dan out of the study or have his treatment changed. She called Olson and tried to see him. She wrote long, detailed letters expressing concerns about everything from Dan's diet and sleep habits to his medications. In total, she sent five letters to Olson and Dr. Charles Schulz—the chairman of the university's psychiatry department and a co-investigator on the CAFE study—communicating her alarm about Dan's condition, especially his inner rage. She received only one reply, dated April 28, from Schulz, who wrote that "it was not clear to me how you thought the treatment team should deal with this issue." Around that time, Mary left a voice message with Jean Kenney, the study coordinator, asking, "Do we have to wait until he kills himself or someone else before anyone does anything?"

Before dawn on the morning of May 8, a police officer and a Catholic priest knocked on Mary's door. Mike Howard, a family friend who lives at her house, answered. Later, in a deposition, Howard described what happened next: "Mary jumped out of her bed and went into the kitchen and stood there, and the priest extended his hand out and said, 'Mary, I'm here to tell you that Dan passed away.' And Mary just literally fell down to her knees and started to shriek and cry, and just started begging, 'Please, no, no, don't let this happen.'"

Dan had stabbed himself to death in the bathtub with a box cutter, ripping open his abdomen and nearly decapitating himself. His body was discovered in the early hours of the morning by a halfway-house worker, along with a note on the nightstand that said, "I left this experience smiling!" Later, when the blind on the study was broken, researchers found that Dan was being treated with Seroquel, the drug manufactured by the study sponsor, AstraZeneca. . . .

In January 2005, the FDA began investigating the circumstances of Dan's suicide. In a report issued that July, before the larger pattern of Seroquel research had begun to emerge, Sharon L. Matson, the FDA investigator, exonerated the university. She wrote, "I did not find any evidence of misconduct, significant violation of the protocol, or regulations governing clinical investigators or IRBs"—the university institutional review board charged with reviewing studies to ensure that they measure up to recognized ethical standards. Matson specifically dismissed the suggestion that Dan was mentally incompetent to consent to the study, writing that "there was nothing different about this subject than others enrolled to indicate that he couldn't provide voluntary, informed consent." (The FDA refused my request to speak with Matson and would not answer questions about the case, citing privacy concerns.) Mary Weiss eventually sued the University of Minnesota, AstraZeneca, Olson, and Schulz, but her case did not even get to trial. District Court Judge John L. Holahan dismissed the suit in 2008 with a partial summary judgment. He ruled that in approving the CAFE study, the university IRB was performing the type of "discretionary function" that is protected from liability under the state's Tort Claims Act. The malpractice suit against Schulz was also dismissed, and the suit against Olson was eventually settled—for $75,000, which Mary says wasn't enough to cover the fees of the expert witnesses her attorneys hired. (Both Schulz and Olson declined to speak about the specifics of the clinical trial or the resulting suit. University spokesman Nick Hanson would say only, "To date, there has been no finding of wrongdoing from any of the investigations or reviews done by the university on this issue.")

The judge also dismissed the case against AstraZeneca. He blasted Mary's lawyers, saying that they had failed to establish that AstraZeneca had a duty to put the interests of research subjects over the interests of the company and the researchers. But he also lamented the lack of case law about clinical trials, saying on this particular point, "Try as it may, this Court's independent research has unearthed not a single case or statute to evidence or support such an alleged duty."

The judge further ruled that Mary's lawyers hadn't shown a causal link between Seroquel and Dan's suicide: An initial drug screening during autopsy had not found any Seroquel in his bloodstream, which suggested that Dan may not have been taking his medication. After the judgment, however, Mary discovered that Seroquel would not be detected in an ordinary drug screening; a special test is required. In the spring of 2008, she called the coroner's office in hopes of getting a special screening for Seroquel. To her surprise, she found that her lawyers and the defendants had already obtained one. The report was dated several days after the summary judgment was issued. It showed 73 nanograms per milliliter of Seroquel in his blood, suggesting that Dan was almost certainly taking the drug, although he may have missed the last scheduled dose before he died.

Disturbing Financial Arrangements

Although Mary's lawsuit was unsuccessful, it revealed some disturbing financial arrangements at the university. As a patient on public assistance, Dan's treatment would have normally generated little income for the university. Under its arrangement with AstraZeneca, however, the psychiatry department earned $15,648 for each subject who completed the CAFE study. In total, the study generated $327,000 for the department. In fact, during the months before Dan was enrolled, the department was apparently feeling pressure from Quintiles, the CRO that managed the study, to step up recruitment. According to emails written by Jean Kenney, the university's study coordinator, the site had been placed on probation for its recruitment problems, and they were still "struggling to get patients." In November 2002, Olson had managed to recruit only one subject in six months. That be-

$350 per Child

If the globalization of clinical trials for adult medications has drawn little attention, foreign trials for children's drugs have attracted even less. The Argentinean province of Santiago del Estero, with a population of nearly a million, is one of the country's poorest. In 2008 seven babies participating in drug testing in the province suffered what the U.S. clinical-trials community refers to as "an adverse event": they died. The deaths occurred as the children took part in a medical trial to test the safety of a new vaccine, Synflorix, to prevent pneumonia, ear infections, and other pneumococcal diseases.

Developed by GlaxoSmithKline, the world's fourth-largest pharmaceutical company in terms of global prescription-drug sales, the new vaccine was intended to compete against an existing vaccine. In all, at least 14 infants enrolled in clinical trials for the drug died during the testing. Their parents, some illiterate, had their children signed up without understanding that they were taking part in an experiment. Local doctors who persuaded parents to enroll their babies in the trial reportedly received $350 per child. The two lead investigators contracted by Glaxo were fined by the Argentinean government. So was Glaxo, though the company maintained that the mortality rate of the children "did not exceed the rate in the regions and countries participating in the study." No independent group conducted an investigation or performed autopsies. As it happens, the brother of the lead investigator in Santiago del Estero was the Argentinean provincial health minister.

Donald L. Barlett and James B. Steele,
"Deadly Medicine," Vanity Fair, *January 2011.*

gan to change in April 2003, when the psychiatry department established a specialized inpatient unit at Fairview Hospital called Station 12, in which every patient could be evaluated for research. By December, Olson had recruited 12 more subjects, including Dan, and Olson had been featured in a CAFE study webcast for "turning an underperforming site into a well-performing site."(Quintiles refused to give comment on the case.)

Olson had another financial reason to maintain good relations with AstraZeneca. According to a disclosure statement for a 2006 conference, he was a member of the AstraZeneca "speaker's bureau," giving paid talks for the company. He had similar arrangements with Eli Lilly and Janssen, the makers of the other atypicals being tested in the CAFE study, as well as Bristol-Myers Squibb and Pfizer. In addition, Olson was working as a paid consultant for Lilly, Janssen, Bristol-Myers Squibb, and Pfizer. Although Olson is not required to disclose how much industry money he received, a public database maintained by the Minnesota pharmacy board indicates that Olson received a total of $240,045 from the pharmaceutical industry between 2002 and 2008, with $149,344 coming from AstraZeneca. Dr. Charles Schulz, his co-investigator and department chair, received an even greater sum: more than $571,000 from the industry, with $112,020 coming from AstraZeneca. The database does not reliably distinguish between payment by drug companies for consulting and speaking, which usually goes directly into a physician's pocket, and research grants, which go to the university and are used to help underwrite the salaries of the grant recipients. (Many academic physicians are required by their universities to generate a substantial portion of their salaries by obtaining research grants.)

In the US, the primary bodies charged with protecting research subjects are known as institutional review boards. According to the University of Minnesota, the purpose of its IRB is to "protect the rights and welfare of human research subjects." However, when the university's IRB officials were deposed under oath, they refused to admit that protecting subjects was their responsibility. "So it's not the institutional review board's purpose to protect clinical trial subjects, is that what you're saying?" asked Gale Pearson, one of the attorneys representing Mary Weiss. "That's true," replied Moira Keane, the director of the IRB. Astonished, Pearson kept returning to the question, to make sure that she understood it correctly. Keane refused to budge. Instead, she claimed that the role of the IRB was to make sure that Olson and the trial sponsor had a plan to protect subjects. (If this were true, it would render IRBs worthless: The sponsor and investigator are the ones that the IRB is supposed to protect subjects *from*.). . .

Highly Misleading

In 2007, the *American Journal of Psychiatry* published the results of the CAFE study. Among the 18 "serious adverse events" recorded for the 400 subjects in the study were an alleged homicide and five suicide attempts, including two successful suicides, both by patients taking Seroquel. (One of these patients, of course, was Dan Markingson.) According to the study authors—three AstraZeneca employees and seven academic physicians, many of whom also consulted for the company—the suicides occurred "despite the close attention provided in clinical research aftercare programs." The authors claimed that the CAFE study showed Seroquel to be of "comparable effectiveness" to Zyprexa and Risperdal for first-episode patients.

According to some experts, the study could hardly have shown otherwise, because it was designed to produce a good result for Seroquel. When I showed the published study to Dr. Peter Tyrer, the editor of the *British Journal of Psychiatry*, he said, "I would have major problems accepting a manuscript of that nature." According to Tyrer, the main problem is the small sample size. Of the 400 subjects enrolled, all but 119 stopped taking the drug before the yearlong study was finished. With so few subjects, the CAFE study was statistically underpowered and thus unlikely to detect any difference in effectiveness between the three drugs. The failure to detect a difference allowed AstraZeneca to claim that Seroquel was as good as the other drugs (or in the language of the study, "non-inferiority"). Tyrer told me, "In scientific terms this study is of very little value."

That's not the only problem. The CAFE study was supposedly designed to test the effectiveness of the three antipsychotics, but the way it did this was by measuring the rate of "all-cause treatment discontinuation," or the percentage of subjects who stopped taking their drug. That is, the CAFE study counted an antipsychotic as "effective" if a subject kept taking it until the end of the study. On the face of it, this type of measurement seems highly misleading; simply because a patient continues to take an antipsychotic does not mean that it is working. Many psychiatrists defend treatment discontinuation as a "pragmatic" way of measuring a drug's overall acceptability, but even by "pragmatic" standards the CAFE study presents a problem. More than 70 percent of subjects in the CAFE study stopped taking their assigned drug, and the most common reason was simply coded as "patient decision." According to Dr. John Davis, the Gillman Professor of psychiatry at the University of Illinois–Chicago, the authors of the CAFE study obscured their results by failing to say *why* patients decided to stop taking the drug—whether patients felt the side effects of the drug were too severe, for example, or if they felt the drug was not working. "It is the hiding of the critical outcomes that gives me pause," he says. "It does not make scientific sense to do a study and not measure one of the most important outcomes."

Yet another problem with the CAFE study is its failure to compare Seroquel to any older antipsychotics. "It's quite a marketing exercise to put all patients in the CAFE study on atypical antipsychotics," says Dr. Glen Spielmans, an associate professor of psychology at Minnesota's Metropolitan State University. "It removes the older drugs from the discussion." One reason AstraZeneca may have done this, he suggests, is that Study 15 had already shown Seroquel to be inferior to the older antipsychotic, Haldol.

Ethical Breach

The bluntest assessment of the study came from Dr. David Healy, a senior psychiatrist at Cardiff University in Wales. Healy is a former consultant to AstraZeneca, among other pharmaceutical companies, and a prominent critic of the industry. "This is a non-study of the worst kind," he said. "It is designed not to pick up a difference between the three drugs. It looks like an entirely marketing-driven exercise."

If these experts are right, then the study in which Dan Markingson committed suicide was not simply a matter of inadequate informed consent, or financial conflicts of interest, or even failure to monitor a subject's care. The ethical breach was built into the study from the start. It is one thing to ask people to take risks for science, or the common good, or to help other people. It is another thing entirely to ask them to risk their lives for the marketing goals of AstraZeneca.

> "There is overwhelming evidence that drug-company influence biases [medical] research itself."

Drug Industry–Sponsored Research Is Biased

Marcia Angell

In the following viewpoint, Marcia Angell claims that clinical trials funded by the pharmaceutical industry are rife with conflicts of interest and biases. She asserts that academic researchers and schools have deals and financial ties with powerful drug companies that sponsor their work. Thus, industry-supported research, she points out, is much more likely to support sponsors' products than is government research. Study biases, Angell contends, include the suppression of negative results and research methods that are designed to produce favorable outcomes for sponsors. The author is a senior lecturer on social medicine at Harvard Medical School and the former editor in chief of the New England Journal of Medicine.

As you read, consider the following questions:

1. How does Angell compare academic medical centers to drug companies?

2. Why do drug companies prefer to work with academic medical centers, in the author's view?

3. In what ways, according to Angell, do clinical trials yield favorable results for sponsors?

In May of 2000, shortly before I stepped down as editor-in-chief of the *New England Journal of Medicine*, I wrote an editorial entitled, "Is Academic Medicine for Sale?" It was prompted by a clinical trial of an antidepressant called Serzone that was published in the same issue of the *Journal*.

The authors of that paper had so many financial ties to drug companies, including the maker of Serzone, that a full-disclosure statement would have been about as long as the article itself, so it could appear only on our Web site. The lead author, who was chairman of the department of psychiatry at Brown University (presumably a full-time job), was paid more than half a million dollars in drug-company consulting fees in just one year. Although that particular paper was the immediate reason for the editorial, I wouldn't have bothered to write it if it weren't for the fact that the situation, while extreme, was hardly unique.

Among the many letters I received in response, two were especially pointed. One asked rhetorically, "Is academic medicine for sale? These days, *everything* is for sale." The second went further: "Is academic medicine for sale? No. The current owner is very happy with it." The author didn't feel he had to say who the current owner was.

The boundaries between academic medicine—medical schools, teaching hospitals, and their faculty—and the pharmaceutical industry have been dissolving since the 1980s, and the important differences between their missions are becoming blurred. Medical research, education, and clinical practice have suffered as a result. Academic medical centers are charged with educating the next generation of doctors, conducting scientifically important research, and taking care of the sickest and neediest patients. That's what justifies their tax-exempt status. In contrast, drug companies—like other investor-owned businesses—are charged with increasing the value of their shareholders' stock. That is their fiduciary responsibility, and they would be remiss if they didn't uphold it. All their other activities are means to that end. The companies are supposed to develop profitable drugs, not necessarily important or innovative ones, and paradoxically enough, the most profitable drugs are the least innovative. Nor do drug companies aim to educate doctors, except as a means to the primary end of selling drugs. Drug companies don't have education budgets; they have marketing budgets from which their ostensibly educational activities are funded. This profound difference in missions is often deliberately obscured—by drug companies because it's good public relations to portray themselves as research and educational institutions, and by academics because it means they don't have to face up to what's really going on.

Industry and Academia

No area of overlap between industry and academia is more important than clinical trials. Unlike basic medical research, which is funded mainly by the National Institutes of Health (NIH), most clinical trials are funded by the pharmaceutical industry. In fact, that is where most pharmaceutical research dollars go. That's because the Food and Drug Administration (FDA) will not approve a drug for sale until it has been tested on human subjects. Pharmaceutical companies must show the FDA that a new drug is reasonably safe and effective, usually as compared with a placebo. That requires clinical trials, in which treatments are compared under rigorous conditions in a sample of the relevant population. The results of drug trials (there may be many) are submitted to the FDA, and if one or two are positive—that is, they show effectiveness without serious risk—the drug is usually approved, even if all the other trials are negative.

Since drug companies don't have direct access to human subjects, they've traditionally contracted with academic researchers to conduct the trials on patients in teaching hospitals and clinics. That practice continues, but over the past couple of decades the terms and conditions have changed dramatically.

Until the mid-1980s, drug companies simply gave grants to medical centers for researchers to test their products, and then waited for the results and hoped their products looked good. Usually the research was investigator-initiated, that is, the question was something the academic researcher thought scientifically important. Sponsors had no part in designing or analyzing the studies, they did not claim to own the data, and they certainly did not write the papers or control publication. Grants were at arm's length.

Thanks to the academy's increasing dependence on industry, that distance is a thing of the past. The major drug companies are now hugely profitable, with net incomes consistently several times the median for *Fortune* 500 companies. In fact, they make more in profits than they spend on research and development (R&D), despite their rhetoric about high prices being necessary to cover their research costs. (They also spend twice as much on marketing and administration as they do on R&D.) The reasons for the astonishing profitability of these companies aren't relevant here, but suffice it to say that as a result the industry has acquired enormous power and influence. In contrast, medical centers have fallen on difficult times (or so they believe), mainly because of shrinking reimbursements for their educational and clinical missions. To a remarkable extent, then, medical centers have become suppliants to the drug companies, deferring to them in ways that would have been unthinkable even twenty years ago.

Often, academic researchers are little more than hired hands who supply human subjects and collect data according to instructions from corporate paymasters. The sponsors keep the data, analyze it, write the papers, and decide whether and when and where to submit them for publication. In multi-center trials, researchers may not even be allowed to see all of the data, an obvious impediment to science and a perversion of standard practice.

While some new companies—called contract research organizations (CROs)—do clinical research for the drug manufacturers by organizing doctors in private practice to enroll their patients in clinical trials, the manufacturers typically prefer to work with academic medical centers. Doing so increases the chances of getting research published, and, more importantly, provides drug companies access to highly influential faculty physicians—referred to by the industry as "thought leaders" or "key opinion leaders." These are the people who write textbooks and medical-journal papers, issue practice guidelines (treatment recommendations), sit on FDA and other governmental advisory panels, head professional societies, and speak at the innumerable meetings and dinners that take place every day to teach clinicians about prescription drugs.

Financial Ties to Companies

In addition to grant support, academic researchers may now have a variety of other financial ties to the companies that sponsor their work. They serve as consultants to the same companies whose products they evaluate, join corporate advisory boards and speakers bureaus, enter into patent and royalty arrangements, agree to be the listed authors of articles ghostwritten by interested companies, promote drugs and devices at company-sponsored symposia, and allow themselves to be plied with expensive gifts and trips to luxurious settings. Many also have equity interest in sponsoring companies.

Much of the time, the institutional conflict-of-interest rules ostensibly designed to control these relationships are highly variable, permissive, and loosely enforced. At Harvard

Conflict of Interest Virtually Impossible to Prove

Unless there is evidence of misconduct (the deliberate misrepresentation of something as fact by someone who knows it is not), it is very difficult to discover and virtually impossible to prove that a piece of biomedical research has been tainted by conflict of interest. No study is perfect, and problems can arise in the labs of even the most conscientious and honest researchers. Biology is enormously complicated anyway, and like all research, biomedical studies begin with choices. Although biomedical research incorporates rigorous scientific rules and is often critically scrutinized by peers, the information can nevertheless be warped—by ending a study because the results are disappointing; changing rules—the protocol or analytic tools—mid-study; not trying to publish negative results; publicizing preliminary results even with final and less positive results in hand; skimming over or even not acknowledging drawbacks; and, especially, casting the results in the best light or, as scientists say, buffing them.

Cynthia Crossen, Tainted Truth:
The Manipulation of Fact in America, *1994.*

Medical School, for example, few conflicts of interest are flatly prohibited; they are only limited in various ways. Like Hollywood, academic medical centers run on a star system, and schools don't want to lose their stars, who are now accustomed to supplementing their incomes through deals with industry.

Schools, too, have deals with industry. Academic leaders, chairs, and even deans sit on boards of directors of drug companies. Many academic medical centers have set up special offices to offer companies quick soup-to-nuts service. Harvard's Clinical Research Institute (HCRI), for example, originally advertised itself as led by people whose "experience gives HCRI an intimate understanding of industry's needs, and knowledge of how best to meet them"—as though meeting industry's needs is a legitimate purpose of an academic institution.

Much of the rationalization for the pervasive research connections between industry and academia rests on the Bayh-Dole Act of 1980, which has acquired the status of holy writ in academia. Bayh-Dole permits—but does not require, as many researchers claim—universities to patent discoveries that stem from government-funded research and then license them exclusively to companies in return for royalties. (Similar legislation applies to work done at the NIH itself.) In this way, academia and industry are partners, both benefiting from public support.

Until Bayh-Dole, all government-funded discoveries were in the public domain. The original purpose of Bayh-Dole was to speed technology transfer from the discovery stage to practical use. It was followed by changes in patent law that loosened the criteria for granting patents. As a consequence, publicly funded discoveries of no immediate practical use can now be patented and handed off to start-up companies for early development. The start-up companies are often founded by the researchers and their institutions, and they usually either license their promising products to larger companies or are bought by large companies outright.

The result of Bayh-Dole was a sudden, huge increase in the number of patents—if not in their quality. And the most prestigious academic centers now have technology-transfer offices and are ringed by start-up companies. Most technology-transfer offices at academic medical centers don't make much money, but every now and then one strikes it rich. Columbia University, for example, received nearly $300 million in royalties from more than 30 biotech companies during the seventeen-year life of its patent on a method for synthesizing biological products. Patenting and licensing the fruits of academic research has the character of a lottery, and everyone wants to play. A less-appreciated outcome of Bayh-Dole is that drug companies no longer have to do their own creative, early-stage research. They can, and increasingly do, rely on universities and start-up companies for that. In fact, the big drug companies now concentrate mainly on the late-stage development of drugs they've licensed from other sources, as well as on producing variations of top-selling drugs already on the market—called "me-too" drugs. There is very little innovative research in the modern pharmaceutical industry, despite its claims to the contrary.

Over the past two or three decades, then, academia and industry have become deeply intertwined. Moreover, these links, though quite recent, are now largely accepted as inherent in medical research. So what's wrong with that? Isn't this just the sort of collaboration that leads to the development of important new medical treatments?

Medical research

Increasingly, industry is setting the research agenda in academic centers, and that agenda has more to do with industry's mission than with the mission of the academy. Researchers and their institutions are focusing too much on targeted, applied research, mainly drug development, and not enough on non-targeted, basic research into the causes, mechanisms, and prevention of disease.

Moreover, drug companies often contract with academic researchers to carry out studies for almost entirely commercial purposes. For example, they sponsor trials of drugs to supplant virtually identical ones that are going off patent. And academic institutions are increasingly focused on the Bayh-Dole lottery. A few years ago, the Dana Farber Cancer Institute sent Harvard faculty an invitation to a workshop called "Forming Science-Based Companies." It began:

> So you want to start a company? Join the Provost, Harvard's Office for Technology and Trademark Licensing (OTTL), leading venture capitalists, lawyers and entrepreneurs for a conference on the basics of forming a start-up based on university technology.

There's a high scientific opportunity cost in serving the aims of the pharmaceutical industry. For example, new antibiotics for treating infections by resistant organisms are an urgent medical need, but are not economically attractive to industry because they are not likely to generate much return on investment.

In addition to distorting the research agenda, there is overwhelming evidence that drug-company influence biases the research itself. Industry-supported research is far more likely to be favorable to the sponsors' products than is NIH-supported research. There are many ways to bias studies— both consciously and unconsciously—and they are by no means always obvious. I saw a good number of them during my two decades as an editor of the *New England Journal of Medicine*. Often, when we rejected studies because of their biases, they turned up in other journals essentially unchanged. And looking back, I now realize that despite our best efforts, we sometimes published biased studies without knowing it. One problem is that we thought that if studies were subjected to rigorous peer review, it was sufficient to disclose authors' commercial ties—essentially to tell readers *caveat emptor* ["let the buyer beware"], as in the Serzone study I mentioned earlier. I no longer believe that's enough.

An important cause of bias is the suppression of negative results. But clinical trials are also biased through research protocols designed to yield favorable results for sponsors. There are many ways to do that. The sponsor's drug maybe compared with another drug administered at a dose so low that the sponsor's drug looks more powerful. Or a drug that's likely to be used by older people will be tested in young people, so that side effects are less likely to emerge. The standard practice of comparing a new drug with a placebo, when the relevant question is how it compares with an existing drug, is also misleading. Supporters of the status quo claim that attempts to regulate conflicts of interest will slow medical advances, but the truth is that conflicts of interest distort medical research, and advances occur *in spite* of them, not because of them.

To be clear, I'm not objecting to all research collaboration between academia and industry—only to terms and conditions that threaten the independence and impartiality essential to medical research. Research collaboration between academia and industry can be fruitful, but it doesn't need to involve payments to researchers beyond grant support. And that support, as I have argued, should be at arm's length.

| "Much research benefiting the public health could not take place without industry dollars."

Research Without Drug Industry Sponsorship May Not Be Feasible

Caroline McGeough

Caroline McGeough is a graduate of Duke University and former editor of its campus newspaper, the Chronicle. *In the following viewpoint, she suggests that the majority of clinical research may not be possible without industry sponsorship. Approximately 70 to 80 percent of clinical research is funded by pharmaceutical and medical device companies, she states, because costs cannot be filled by government agencies alone. Also, McGeough speculates, some academic research organizations use policy and practice to shape the degree to which bias and conflicts of interest can enter studies.*

As you read, consider the following questions:

1. How does McGeough describe academic research organizations and compare them with contract research organizations?

2. What is the conflict of interest policy at Duke University's School of Medicine, as described by the author?

3. As cited by McGeough, how do John March and Robert Harrington view public-private partnerships?

In one tower of a nondescript, nine-story white building on Fulton Street [in Durham, North Carolina], just across from Duke University Hospital, operates the world's largest academic clinical research institute, generating more than $125 million in revenue per year from the research grants and contracts it receives from both government sources and from industry. Its more than 218 clients in the pharmaceutical and medical device sectors include corporate giants Johnson & Johnson, Pfizer, GlaxoSmithKline and GE Healthcare. The Duke Clinical Research Institute [DCRI], composed of more than 1,000 employees supporting the worldwide clinical research projects directed by 220 Duke faculty [members], has evolved from a small cardiological research outfit in 1996 into an enterprise capable of conducting large-scale Phase I through Phase IV clinical trials across 20 therapeutic areas.

"There's no other university that presents the full translational continuum in a way that blends the professionalism that you find in industry with the expertise and mission of an academic health center, in the way that Duke does," said Dr. John March, director of neurosciences medicine at DCRI and professor of psychiatry and psychology at the School of Medicine.

In the contracts with pharmaceutical and medical device companies that provided DCRI with 67 percent of its funding in 2009, the Institute arranges to perform a range of core clinical research services—including study design, accessing patient populations and project management and execution—typically in exchange for the company providing funding or materials for the study. Of all U.S. academic institutions, Duke receives the most industry funding annually for its research and development—$152 million in 2008, according to National Science Foundation data—primarily because of DCRI's revenue-generating power. The School of Medicine, and the University as a whole, benefit from a yearly inflow of revenue from DCRI's funding agreements. "In a world where society is distrustful of the motives of the pharmaceutical and medical device world, it is in everybody's best interests—society, the industry, the academic community—to have some independence over the conduct of research," said Dr. Robert Harrington, director of DCRI, explaining his sales pitch to pharmaceutical and medical device companies.

But as a recipient of high-value funding grants from corporations, who have a significant stake in a positive outcome for trials involving their products, DCRI is particularly vulnerable to the major risks posed by financial conflicts of interest—or, formally defined, when a researcher or institution's own economic interests contradict professional obligation. The financial ties criss-crossing the once-rigid barrier between academia and industry are many and complex, inclusive of receiving payment for consulting or research services provided to a company, and holding equity or intellectual property rights in a company—practices now ubiquitous among clinical researchers.

As collaboration between academia and industry in clinical research becomes more common and more lucrative, some warn that unaddressed financial conflicts of interest will erode the objectivity of the science and menace the welfare of clinical trial participants. Critics point to scandals like the one that erupted in 1999 over the death of 18-year-old Jesse Gelsinger, a patient enrolled in a gene therapy experiment led by a principal investigator who had founded a biotechnology company that stood to profit from the experiment's success. They warn that a proposal offered by industry and accepted by academic clinical research—with the union sweetened with funding contracts—will undermine the credibility of academia's findings. "Our problem, nationally, is that our research is so biased with financial interest that the scandals that plague the financial world are every bit as ubiquitous and serious in medicine," said Jeanne Lenzer, an investigative journalist who has contributed to the *British Medical Journal, Slate* and *The Atlantic* on conflicts of interest in clinical research. "You pull back the bed covers and what we're finding, over and over again, is not only that patients in clinical trials are not being protected, but that when bias gets into the science, it puts all of us at risk."

A Different Breed

Supporters of academia-industry collaborations argue that much research benefiting the public health could not take place without industry dollars, and that regulatory controls are in place to mitigate bias. A case study in commercialized academic clinical research, DCRI sits at the center of a broader debate over the propriety of using private dollars to support a discipline whose results impact public welfare at large.

Contract research organizations—or CROs, which perform clinical research services for industry or public agencies—emerged in the 1980s to capitalize on the trend toward outsourcing clinical trials once performed by pharmaceutical or medical device company staff. Targeting greater efficiency and cost reduction during the trial phases, the outsourced model has now become dominant practice in the pharmaceutical industry, with some retaining only their management teams, March said. The CRO market has grown at a break-neck speed, with annual industry revenue climbing from $7 billion in 2001 to $17.8 billion in 2007, according to a 2007 *New England Journal of Medicine* study. Three of the four largest CROs named in the study—Quintiles, Covance and Charles River Laboratories—are located in the Raleigh-Durham [North Carolina] area. Media reports about mismanaged clinical trials run by CROs, such as the 2005 SFBC International trial in Florida involving Hispanic immigrants with limited knowledge of the study's risks, have prompted questions about the organizations' qualifications, ethics and degree of independence from corporate sponsors.

But academic research organizations (AROs) like DCRI are a different breed from companies like Quintiles, as Harrington was quick to emphasize. Typically housed within universities and run by faculty, AROs are sheltered from the allegations against professional credibility that dog CROs, yet are still not immune to the question of intellectual independence from commercial sponsors of research. Harrington spoke with gentle condescension toward CROs, which he says treat research as a commodity to be exchanged in a transaction, rather than an endeavor intended to advance a broader institutional goal. "We're not here to do contract research," Harrington said. "We're here to do research that furthers our mission."

Although DCRI is often asked to be the "arms and legs" of a trial, merely implementing a trial that has already been designed, Harrington said DCRI avoids participating in this type of study and instead seeks to collaborate as an equal partner in research projects. March, however, said there are still some occasions when DCRI does basic contract research, though it has never agreed to execute a research protocol that faculty thought might tarnish its ethical reputation.

"If someone wants to do something a particular way, and it's their program of research and they're paying for it, we go along with it. But if we think it's unethical, and for whatever reason the flaw of the protocol is so egregious that we wouldn't participate, we wouldn't do it," March said. "But I can't think of a single example of that over the past 25 years."

Confronting Bias

As a scientific research organization that relies on funding from corporate sponsors, DCRI routinely confronts the possibility of significant bias in its research, reacting to a fundamental conflict of interest. Although those involved in the study seek scientific impartiality, those underwriting the study seek a certain partiality toward the company's own products, which are usually the subject of the research it sponsors. "Most industry-funded research is to achieve an end, which is usually defined as more reasons to use a given drug. It's our job as academics to be the brokers—what are the right questions to be asked, and how can we ask this?" said Dr. Ross McKinney, director of the Trent Center for Bioethics and chair of School of Medicine and University conflict of interest committees. "My worry is that we lose that ability to be the honest broker, because we start to get a stake in the economic benefits that come from more drug sales."

Financial conflicts of interest in clinical research pose two main risks: to the objectivity of the science and to the welfare of the patients. Although no reliable data is available on how financial conflicts of interest impact individual patient welfare, strong data suggests that conflicts challenge the integrity of the science, said Dr. Kevin Weinfurt, a medical psychologist at DCRI and lead author on several studies examining conflicts of interest in medicine. A 1998 report in the *New England Journal of Medicine*, for example, found that studies that positively reviewed a treatment for cardiovascular disorder were overwhelmingly authored by researchers with financial stakes in the treatment's manufacturers. (Ninety-six percent of authors had such interests, vs. 60 percent and 37 percent for neutral and critical authors, respectively.)

The influence of bias in professional contexts is often subtle and nebulous and, at times, exerted without the person's intent. But financial biases differ from personal and other biases in one important way, as Lenzer pointed out: They are always unidirectional, pointed favorably toward the source of income. Furthermore, attempts at regulating bias among researchers may come off as an affront on their integrity as scientists.

"We often meet with people when there's a significant conflict, and they say, 'How can you say that some amount of money can influence me more than providing care for patients? You are demeaning me by accusing me of being influenced by these external relationships,'" McKinney said. "When you look at their data, their opinions are bullshit. It doesn't hold water. In fact, we are influenced."

Institutional policy and practice lay down rules governing some types of financial conflicts of interest among researchers, which shape the degree to which such biases can enter into research. "Conflicts of interest must be defined, disclosed and eliminated when they are avoidable or particularly threatening, and managed if there is no other option," said Marilyn Field, a National Academy of Sciences researcher who authored a book on conflicts of interest in medicine. Several recent reviews of U.S. academic medical centers, however, have found substantial variations in conflict of interest policy, and judged most to be insufficient.

Benchmarked against its peers, McKinney said, Duke's policy requires more vigorous reporting of financial interests than those of other institutions, protecting from the influence of bias and damage to the University's good name. The School of Medicine's 2008 conflict of interest policy mandates reporting to the Conflict of Interest Office financial interests in excess of $600, and it requires a management plan for interests between $10,000 and $25,000. Researchers with financial relationships exceeding $25,000 are banned from participation as a lead principal investigator in a study related to that company or its products. Those researchers would still be eligible to participate in the study in a different capacity.

In addition, DCRI enables its researchers to voluntarily disclose potential conflicts of interest—a measure Harrington, whose own disclosure form inventories financial relationships with 15 corporations, says is relatively unique among clinical research organizations. About half of the 95 faculty financially supported by DCRI have opted to publicly disclose, said Kristen O'Berry, director of faculty finance and administration at DCRI. Although O'Berry said she was unsure why some faculty did not opt to disclose their financial relationships, Weinfurt said researchers may be loath to fill out additional forms or have privacy concerns regarding how the public would interpret the information. Although it is useful to set certain dollar-based thresholds for disclosure of researchers' financial relationships, research suggests that bias can influence decisions even when the economic stakes are small, Field said. "We don't know a lot about the way in which that kind of bias might occur," she said. "For example if you had a nice visit with a drug company representative, perhaps there's a greater potential for that physician to use the drug represented by that company."

Another vital component to the protection of scientific integrity in industry-funded clinical research concerns which intellectual property rights the research organization guards. DCRI fiercely protects its rights to access data and to publish the results of research in contractual language, Harrington said, indicating its intent to carefully manage the data and show confidence in association with its results.

Public-Private Collaboration

When March looks toward the future of biotechnological research, he sees the dominant model as a public-private collaboration, where clinical research institutes like DCRI carry out studies with funding from both governmental agencies and corporations to explore shared areas of interest. "We have to find a way of making this work, and we have to do it in a transparent and ethical way," he said. "Otherwise we'll be doomed to the ethical lapses of the past, and that will encourage people to divorce research completely from industry funding."

Harrington noted an example of a typical DCRI study that fits the public-private vision March had elaborated. DCRI performed a large randomized trial whose operations were funded by the National Heart, Lung and Blood Institute to determine whether implanting a defibrillator would reduce risk of death in patients with heart damage. The defibrillator devices, which cost around $75,000 each, were provided by Medtronic, a medical device company that manufactures several types of implantable defibrillators.

"If, in fact, the defibrillator was shown to be superior to no defibrillator, that obviously has potential marketing implications for the company," Harrington said. "They now have something that's been done independently of them, so it raises the credibility of the research that then might benefit them." The trial, whose results were published in 2005 in the *New England Journal of Medicine*, found that single-chamber implantable cardioverter defibrillators reduced the rate of sudden death within five years by 23 percent, as compared with a placebo or a drug that corrects abnormal heart rhythms.

Both Harrington and March view these public-private partnerships, which tend to grow organically through researchers' contacts in the industry, as mutually beneficial arrangements. The public gains academically-verified knowledge about the efficacy of certain drugs or devices, and the private company gains an evaluation that—if positive—can be used to market their products. Although supportive of the consortia model, McKinney emphasized that strict ground rules need to be set to prevent private funding sources from overriding the public interest—which, as a tax-exempt institution, Duke is obliged to represent.

But Lenzer, terming the intermingling of public and private funding for clinical research a contamination of the science, noted that in some jointly-funded studies, the resulting data is owned by the participating university, unavailable even through a Freedom of Information Act request. "We have to increase public funding that is not combined with private funding, and there should be comparative effectiveness studies," Lenzer said. "Without that, we're really lost."

One provision of the health care reform bill will shed more light on the degree of financial involvement between academia and industry by requiring American drug, device, biologics and medical supplies manufacturers to disclose payments made to physicians and teaching hospitals. Public disclosure of these records, which will start in 2013, McKinney said, may make industry "cagey" about its routine payments, though Lenzer doubted that the public would know what to make of the data.

Most sources, however, said governmental agencies would never be able to fill the funding void that would open up if industry and academia divorced—particularly in clinical research, where an estimated 70 to 80 percent is funded by industry. To remove or greatly reduce the amount of industry money flowing through clinical research would cripple the funding system and make it difficult for companies to harvest the expertise of clinical researchers. "To remove industry sponsorship of individual studies would obviously create a pretty huge hole in clinical research right now," Weinfurt said. "This is just how research is getting done. You can try to change the system, but that is going to take an awful lot of time."

Periodical and Internet Sources Bibliography

The following articles have been selected to supplement the diverse views presented in this chapter.

Michael Caliguiri	"For Continued Success of Clinical Trials, Insurance Coverage for Routine Medical Costs Is Needed," *Oncology Times*, November 25, 2008.
Patricia F. Dimond	"The Problem of Insufficient Reporting and Publication Bias," *GEN*, November 22, 2010.
Marilyn Elias	"Conflicts of Interest Bedevil Psychiatric Drug Research," *USA Today*, June 3, 2009.
Farhad Handjani	"Monitoring Clinical Trials: A Gratifying Experience," *Journal of the European Medical Writers Association*, vol. 17, no. 1, 2008.
Amy Harmon	"New Drugs Stir Debate on Rules of Clinical Trials," *New York Times*, September 18, 2010.
Jonah Lerher	"The Truth Wears Off," *New Yorker*, December 13, 2010.
Gary C. Messplay and D. Kyle Sampson	"Clinical Trials Code of Conduct: Protecting Human Subjects and Preserving Research Integrity," *Contract Pharma*, September 2009.
Steven Miles and Jeff Stier	"Point/Counterpoint: Does Pharmaceutical Industry Funding Bias Research?," *Internal Medicine News*, February 15, 2009.
Dennis Normile	"The Promise and Pitfalls of Clinical Trials Overseas," *Science*, October 10, 2008.
Ed Silverman	"Out of Sight," *Portfolio*, October 5, 2009.

OPPOSING
VIEWPOINTS®
SERIES

CHAPTER 2

Does the FDA Effectively Regulate Prescription Drugs?

Chapter Preface

An estimated 150 hospital drugs are in low supply in 2011—three times the figure in 2006—according to the American Society of Health-System Pharmacists. More than a third of these are deemed "medically necessary" by federal officials, including antibiotics, anesthetics used in surgery, and cancer-fighting treatments. "These are the worst shortages I have ever seen," observes Thomas Wheeler, director of pharmacy for Advocate Illinois Masonic Medical Center in Chicago. "The most troubling aspect is that it is critical drugs for which there are limited alternatives,"[1] he notes.

One cause of drug shortages is the stricter control of quality under the Food and Drug Administration (FDA) in the last few years. "The quality issues can range from finding toxins and 'particulate matter' in medicines to workers inaccurately filling out the required paperwork to verify that the drugs, as well as the devices used to intravenously deliver the products to patients, are safe and effective," states health reporter Bruce Japsen. "Even after a company restarts production of a drug, it takes time for a plant to catch up to the back orders,"[2] he adds.

To address this problem, US senators Amy Klobuchar and Bob Casey introduced the Preserving Access to Life-Saving Medications Act in February 2011. It would require manufacturers to notify the FDA much sooner of any event or circumstance that would result in a drug shortage. "Physicians, pharmacists, and patients are currently among the last to know when an essential drug will no longer be available—that's not right," maintains Klobuchar. "This common-sense solution

1. Quoted in Bruce Japsen, "Drug Shortages Cause Hospitals to Use Older Types of Medicines," *Los Angeles Times*, February 21, 2011. http://articles.latimes.com/print/2011/feb/21/business/la-fi-drug-shortage-20110221.
2. Japsen, "Drug Shortages."

will help set up an early warning system so pharmacists and physicians can prepare in advance and ensure that patients continue to receive the best care possible."[3] However, critics insist that it would burden manufacturers with more regulation. "And how, exactly, will notifying the FDA help with the shortage?" a commenter asks on Overlawyered, a legal website. "And what if the 'factor' that's causing the shortage is the FDA's rules themselves—will the company find itself facing investigation and retaliation if it is perceived as blaming the FDA for the shortage?"[4] In the following chapter, the authors debate whether the FDA's regulation of pharmaceuticals is effective.

3. Office of Amy Klobuchar, "Klobuchar, Casey Introduce Bill to Address Unprecedented Prescription Drug Shortages," February 7, 2011. http://klobuchar.senate.gov/newsreleases_detail.cfm?id=330941&.
4. Walter Olson, "Widespread Shortages of Hospital Drugs," Overlawyered, March 2, 2011.

> "The [FDA's] mission is to promote and protect the public health by ensuring that safe and effective drugs are available to Americans."

FDA Regulation Ensures Drug Safety and Effectiveness

Janet Woodcock, as told to the FDA

In the following viewpoint, Janet Woodcock claims that the regulatory practices of the Food and Drug Administration (FDA) and its Center of Drug Evaluation and Research (CDER) ensure the safety and effectiveness of drugs. She declares that the center's drug review process is efficient and timely, cutting approval times in half. Also, the FDA has stepped in to test medications incorrectly deemed useful by physicians, to give seriously ill patients early access to promising treatments, and to approve off-label uses, Woodcock explains. For the future, she continues, the administration is adapting to the emergence of managed care, resistance to antibiotics, and drug development for chronic diseases. Woodcock is deputy commissioner for operations at the FDA, a federal agency of the US Department of Health and Human Services.

Janet Woodcock, "A Conversation About the FDA and Drug Regulation with Janet Woodcock," FDA.org, May 28, 2009. www.fda.gov.

As you read, consider the following questions:

1. What is the CDER's accelerated approval procedure, in Woodcock's words?

2. As stated by the author, how does the FDA guide the safe off-label uses of drugs?

3. In Woodcock's opinion, why may testing not detect all of a drug's potential problems?

FDA: *What is the mission of the Center for Drug Evaluation and Research [CDER]?*

Janet Woodcock: CDER's mission is to promote and protect the public health by ensuring that safe and effective drugs are available to Americans. This is a very succinct mission statement, but it encompasses a lot of activities.

What are the public's expectations of drug regulation?

The public's expectations—and the drug regulatory system that meets them—have been evolving over the course of the last 100 years. Since the early part of the last century, the public's basic expectations have been that all marketed drugs should be effective and safe within the context of their use and that unsafe or ineffective drugs should be kept off the market.

Another long-standing expectation of people is that human drugs should be of high quality, because poor-quality drugs threatened the lives of many Americans early in the 20th century. Also, there had been cases of false and flagrant claims made for drugs, as well as false and misleading advertising. Americans expect the system to take care of that.

A more recent imperative is that the drug regulatory system must allow generic competition to help maintain reasonable prices for drugs and to help control health care costs. Clearly, it is an expectation of various groups that the generic industry should flourish and that it should set a standard for drug pricing in the United States.

Over the past 15 years or so, it has become very important to many Americans that seriously ill patients who lack treatment alternatives should have access to investigational drugs. Another expectation that is becoming more widespread is that all patient advocacy groups should have information about how to use approved drugs. For example, there should be information available on how to use drugs for children. Use of approved drugs should be studied enough in children so that pediatric information and, perhaps, specific formulations are available. Also, there are growing expectations that information about drugs—targeted at specific vulnerable populations such as the elderly and women—will be made available, and that the drug regulatory system will somehow make this happen.

Finally, Americans realize that while it is important to keep unsafe and ineffective drugs off the market, a robust and flourishing drug development research program is also necessary in this country. Americans expect the drug regulatory system will get drugs through the pipeline, make them available to patients rapidly, and ensure all studies on human subjects are ethical and safe.

Service to the Public

What has the CDER done to improve service to the public?

For a long time, people lauded the quality of the CDER drug review process, but criticized it for being too slow. The FDA began to address the issue in 1993 with the establishment of user fees. Since the industry is receiving a service from the government through CDER's review of its marketing applications, many felt industry should contribute directly toward the costs of the review process. Congress, industry, and the FDA negotiated the user fee program. Industry pays fees to add to the FDA's resources for reviewing new drug applications. In exchange, the FDA makes a commitment to meet certain goals for review times.

The CDER has been meeting all those goals. In fact, it has exceeded almost all of the goals, and it expects to continue to exceed them. Basically, the review times have been cut in half. The program has been so successful that it has been renewed for two more five-year terms. The approval process has been further improved by CDER's accelerated approval procedure. Under this procedure, drugs for serious and life-threatening diseases can be approved earlier in the process. The CDER does this on the condition that there are indicators—called surrogate endpoints—that can allow us to reasonably predict that the drug will provide some benefit. The manufacturer still must continue clinical testing after the drug is made available, but patients with life-threatening diseases benefit by getting the drugs they need faster.

For instance, under this program, the CDER approved the protease inhibitors used to treat HIV infection. Many Americans who have started therapy with these drugs have had their health restored to them and have returned to productive lives. All the protease inhibitors were approved in a matter of months; one was approved in only 42 days. A major decline in AIDS-related deaths in the United States is partly attributed to the availability of these drugs.

What assurance does the public have that FDA regulation will be balanced?

I believe quite strongly that a democratic government has to be fair. It's one of the principles of our society. One of the reasons that the citizens are willing to give power to the government is that the government is perceived as being fair and just. This requires balanced regulation, and that is why I have emphasized consistency in regulatory matters and policy, professionalism, and evenhandedness.

I also feel that human beings work together better in a nonadversarial manner. An adversarial relationship, although sometimes necessary, is not the best way to conduct public affairs. It wastes a lot of resources, and it doesn't get the best results. A byproduct of working closely with industry, consumer groups, Congress, and the public is that you are much more likely to get balanced regulation.

In the regulatory area, we are talking about the exercise of federal power over other citizens in this country. It requires professionalism, tact, diplomacy, and a whole set of skills that may not be required in other areas.

Consumer Decisions

Why not trust consumers to decide for themselves which medicines work for them?

I don't think it's in the government's best interest to stand between people—especially those who are desperately ill—and their desire to take particular medicines. But this libertarian issue shouldn't be confused with the scientific issue of whether patients can tell what medicines work, because with almost any drug treatment we use today, they can't tell.

Doctors thought for years they could tell what worked. In the 1960s, for example, doctors were convinced that diethylstilbestrol, or DES, was terrific for preventing early miscarriages, and they gave it to thousands of women in pregnancy. "The women had miscarriages before, and I put them on this DES, and some of them didn't have miscarriages. So obviously, it's very effective," doctors thought. In fact, when DES was actually subjected to scientific testing, it had no effect on miscarriage whatsoever. Not only was it absolutely ineffective, but unfortunately, it had delayed negative health effects on the fetus.

We had a more recent experience like this with a heart rhythm drug. After people have heart attacks, they can have extra beats. And it's known that a percentage of people with those extra beats will have sudden death. Well, drugs were discovered that made the sudden beats go away, and people thought, "Wonderful! Make the beats go away, and sudden death will go away." The medicine became the standard of practice throughout the United States; everybody was using the drug.

There were some skeptics at the National Institutes of Health [NIH] and the FDA who said the drug ought to be tested. The NIH set up a trial, and what they discovered shocked everyone: Yes, the drugs make the beats go away, but the people who were put on the drugs had sudden death at a substantially higher rate than the people who were just left having the beats. The drugs actually made the problem worse, and maybe more likely to occur.

Even the people who did the trial were later haunted by the fact that they had given some people that drug. They were people whom the researchers knew, and some of them died. So the answer is, many, many very smart people have thought they knew what drugs would help them and what drugs would hurt them, and clinical tests again and again have proven them wrong. They didn't know.

What is there to lose by giving people with life-threatening diseases like AIDS and terminal cancer access to whatever drugs they want?

If we didn't test drugs—if people could take whatever drug they wanted without any testing—there would be no way to tell whether any of the thousands, millions, of candidate drugs out there worked. So no one would ultimately benefit.

For people with life-threatening illnesses, even the patient groups don't agree on where the right balance is between identifying treatments that will really improve patients' health and allowing people to have immediate access to experiment with drugs that might work for them.

I think AIDS is a good example. We had a lot of discussions with the AIDS activists early on about access to treatments. The FDA put together many programs to allow people early access to those drugs even before they were approved.

But at the same time, companies pursued testing to see whether these agents worked. Ultimately, some drugs were dropped because they didn't work or because they were so toxic that the risks outweighed the benefits. Ultimately, good drugs were found and then approved by the CDER.

Now we're decreasing mortality with HIV. So every person with HIV has a path of drugs to take that he or she knows will work to improve health and has been proven to do so. If we'd gone down the other path, and everyone had been able to try anything with no testing, we'd still be at the same point so much later into the epidemic: Everyone would have total availability to all drugs, but we wouldn't know what worked.

Some of the AIDS activists have actually told us they want more rigorous testing because, as they study their disease and the treatments, they realize they need information to make choices about which drugs they should take, even among the approved drugs. They want the CDER to mandate a greater number of big trials that would include combination therapy. "What if I start this combination early, versus if I take this single drug first? Which would help me to be in better health 10 years from now?" Those are the kinds of questions they want answered, and you can't answer those questions unless you do scientific testing.

Off-Label Use and Clinical Testing

Isn't the CDER infringing on drug marketers' freedom of speech when the agency restricts what is said in drug labeling and advertising?

There is a category of speech called "commercial speech," used when you're making a sales pitch. So, although some other kinds of speech are less restricted, things that are promotional in nature may have certain constraints legitimately put on them.

For example, drug labeling and advertising must be balanced about a drug's risks and benefits and not be misleading. In my opinion, consumers want truthful information, not hype.

Because people would like to receive all the latest information about a drug from the manufacturer, there has been a lot of debate about uses that are considered "off-label"—not approved by the CDER. Obviously, medical science doesn't happen in spurts, but continuously. After a drug is put on the market, health professionals continuously experiment with new uses. We think that is appropriate and don't want to restrict that kind of use of drugs. But we don't want manufacturers to promote these uses to consumers until they are proven safe and effective.

The FDA Modernization Act of 1997 allows manufacturers to provide physicians with articles from scientific journals and textbooks about new uses if they are conducting a study on the drug's new use or they promise to conduct one in the near future. To help the situation, we've put out a guidance document on how much information a manufacturer needs in order to get a new use on the label. We are also being very aggressive in getting new uses approved for people who were traditionally excluded from drug testing—children, women of child-bearing age, and the elderly. New uses have been approved in the last 10 years at more than double the rate they were approved previously. We think that manufacturers are motivated to submit applications for new uses because they know that we have been approving them promptly if they are found to work. . . .

Is the center's rapid approval of drugs compromising public safety?

Everybody has to be aware that the clinical testing—the premarket testing of drugs—will not detect all the problems. It just can't. It won't detect some of the problems with the drug or some of the toxicities with some drugs. This fact is something that the public and the medical and pharmacy communities really need to understand better.

Why doesn't testing detect them all? Well, it isn't because the review process breaks down. First of all, it's because some of the events are rare. They may occur in one out of 10,000 people. So, if you test 5,000 people in your clinical development program, you probably won't see it. Even if you test 10,000, you may not see it; or if you see it, you wouldn't believe it was related. We know this is going to happen sometimes after a drug is approved.

Second, some problems with drugs are caused by the way they're used outside of the parameters for which they're approved. I think the diet drug fenfluramine is a good example. It caused heart-valve problems. It was only approved for three months' use, but people used it for longer periods of time.

Also, sometimes we encounter errors in the use of the drug; for example, medication errors that were hard to foresee prior to approval. Maybe the name, even though we look at the names, was too close to another drug name, and once they get out on the market, they get mixed up.

For all these reasons, a vigorous program is needed after drugs are marketed, to detect these safety problems and to correct them as soon as possible. We have a spontaneous reporting system through which people can report all these problems to the agency. We get a tremendous number of reports—about a quarter million a year.

We are upgrading this system. Because it has a very large number of reports, it is hard to deal with them all. We're totally computerizing this, and with the industry, we're trying to move toward electronic submission of all reports. This will help us analyze them faster and disseminate information better.

Role of Tomorrow's FDA

What's in the future?

First, we are moving toward a completely electronic submission and review environment. A typical drug application can take so much paper that we need a forklift to transfer it. With electronic submissions, we are able to fit it all on a CD-ROM or two. This means less paperwork for everyone and quicker, more accurate reviews.

Second, I think the CDER is really going to have to step up to the plate in the new world of medical care, where managed care is the paradigm of how patients are being taken care of in this country. We need to think about how our information and how our role of drug approval and regulation fit in with the newly emerging health care system in the United States.

How does the pharmaceutical firm's role in the managed-care industry fit with the FDA's traditional method of regulating what pharmaceutical firms can say about their drugs? This, again, is a very controversial issue. The public has a lot of issues about having their medicines switched.

Antibiotic resistance is something you'll be hearing about in upcoming years. We're getting to the point where we have new, effective antibiotics that may be the only antibiotic that can treat a certain bug. Should this antibiotic be allowed to be administered widely throughout the country to the point where it, too, has resistance developed to it? What should be the national approach to this upcoming problem of antibiotic resistance?

More and more drug development is aimed at treating chronic diseases. We can't ask drug developers to study a drug for the entire lifetime of a patient with a chronic disease. They may study it for one or two years total per patient. So what should we do after that drug is approved? How much information should be collected, and what happens if you take the drug for 5 years, or 10 years, or 20 years? What should we do? And what power should we have to compel that kind of information to be collected?

Finally, in my opinion, effective communication is linked to drug safety. If we can get the information about potential or actual problems with drugs out to doctors, patients, and those people who need it, then drugs are going to be safer. If people are in the dark, then misuse of drugs will occur more frequently. We are working toward improving prescription drug labeling and improving over-the-counter drug labeling.

Most people cannot have missed the increased prominence of direct-to-consumer advertising recently. In addition, there's a private, ongoing, voluntary process to have consumer information available at the pharmacy for prescription drugs. So when consumers fill their prescriptions, they will receive information sheets. This process is being monitored by the FDA to ensure that it happens adequately. This is a very important issue for drug safety: that consumers get adequate information on how to use their drugs and that the information they get is correct.

> "Drugs safely and effectively used by thousands of consumers in other countries for years were kept off the market in this country [because of FDA regulation]."

FDA Regulation Delays the Approval of Beneficial Drugs

Tomas J. Philipson and Eric Sun

Tomas J. Philipson is chairman of Project FDA at the Manhattan Institute for Policy Research, a think tank based in New York. Eric Sun is an anesthesiology resident at Stanford University School of Medicine. In the following viewpoint, the authors contend that Food and Drug Administration (FDA) testing and approvals delay the entry of beneficial drugs to the market. Philipson and Sun draw attention to the FDA error of withholding the release of safe and effective medications, which may lead distressed patients to obtain them abroad or illegally. Additionally, the authors claim that premarket testing may reveal little about the adverse effects of drugs for the general population and not include various uses prescribed by physicians.

Tomas J. Philipson and Eric Sun, "Cost of Caution: The Impact on Patients of Delayed Drug Approvals," *Project FDA Report*, vol. 2, June 2010. Copyright © 2010 Manhattan Institute for Policy Research, Inc. All rights reserved. Reproduced with permission.

As you read, consider the following questions:

1. In the authors' opinion, why do economists and policy analysts believe that the FDA is overly cautious in drug approvals?

2. Why are the benefits of an exhaustive review process not as extensive as assumed, in Philipson and Sun's opinion?

3. What would have been the benefits of approving of medications for HIV/AIDS, lymphoma, and breast cancer three years earlier, according to the authors?

The FDA's [Food and Drug Administration's] mission is not only to bring safe and effective drugs to market but, as it notes in its mission statement, to help "speed innovations that make medicines and foods more effective, safer, and more affordable." In almost every decision that the FDA makes, it has to confront the trade-off between safety and availability, since no drug or medical device is safe for everyone under all circumstances. Delaying access to new drugs by requiring companies to conduct additional tests or clinical trials may allow the agency time to accumulate more evidence on the drug's safety, but it also slows access to the drug by patients who might benefit from it. Conversely, expedited access may expose consumers to unknown risks.

But the harm that results from delaying or denying access to a beneficial treatment is less apparent than the harm that occurs when a drug producing serious side effects is mistakenly approved for sale. Accordingly, an excessively cautious FDA is likely to be considered by policymakers and the public no worse than prudent, while regulators will be judged careless (or worse) when rare side effects emerge and harm patients. For these reasons, many economists and policy analysts believe that the FDA usually errs on the side of caution, even though such a policy may result in greater suffering than a more active or lenient one. [The Manhattan Institute's James] Copland and [Paul] Howard elaborate:

> "Type I" error [involves] approving a drug as reasonably safe that later turns out to be unsafe or ineffective; and "Type II" error [involves] withholding from the public a drug that is reasonably safe and effective.

> The Type I error, insofar as it results in widely publicized deaths or serious injuries after a drug is approved for sale, is of greater public concern and consequently has the greater impact on agency oversight by Congress. Exemplifying the Type I error is the history of thalidomide, a sedative that was widely marketed in Europe and Japan (but not the United States) to treat pregnancy-related nausea ("morning sickness") before it was discovered that it caused severe birth defects. The thalidomide tragedy led in 1962 to passage of the Kefauver Harris Amendment, which created what became the FDA's current drug-approval regime.

Although no one can deny that the FDA's caution in evaluating thalidomide prevented the tragedies that occurred overseas from repeating themselves here, it is also the case that since the thalidomide affair, other drugs safely and effectively used by thousands of consumers in other countries for years were kept off the market in this country, forcing prudent but needy Americans to obtain these drugs abroad or illegally import them.

Growing awareness of Type II errors throughout the 1970s and 1980s, particularly in the case of drugs treating life-threatening illnesses such as AIDS and cancer, eventually led to congressional and FDA reforms designed to accelerate agency review of certain types of treatments. These reforms recognized that the good that such drugs could do for particularly distressed patients lacking effective alternatives exceeded the harm that could be caused by exposing those patients to drugs with unknown side effects.

More broadly, it might be the case that the collective good that helpful drugs do substantially exceeds the collective harm inflicted by unsafe drugs that make it to market and may have been hurried there. For instance, one study found that acceleration of the FDA's review of new drug applications facilitated by user fees created by the 1992 Prescription Drug User Fee Act (PDUFA) found that the benefits of added speed outweighed costs by a substantial margin—even if all harms caused by drugs approved after the law was passed were blamed on the legislation. The authors write that the benefits of added speed, even after such an assumption was made, outweighed costs by at least three to one. The authors suggest that "the value of accelerated review was so great that one must ask whether additional measures—that actually did allow more bad drugs to make the cut—would be justified."

Every drug presents its own unique regulatory challenges, of course, and it is impossible to predict benefits or risks with complete confidence. But by expanding the FDA's resources to review new drug applications, one of the steps pursued under the PDUFA, the agency was able to substantially reduce the backlog of drugs awaiting regulatory review without any impact on either the rate of drug withdrawals or the time it took to withdraw them. Another reason to favor the expedition of reviews and approvals is that drugs producing unacceptable numbers of serious side effects among the public at large are likely to be quickly discovered and withdrawn, while a beneficial drug does good for years and years, or at least until such time as an even better drug supersedes it.

Additional FDA reforms, coming under the general heading of "accelerated approval," reflected a willingness to approve new drugs earlier in the drug-development process, on the strength of "surrogate" markers suggesting that they were "reasonably likely . . . to predict clinical benefit." Under these standards, a drug that was likely to be effective against a given

Lost Societal Benefits Are Unknown

Although they can profoundly compromise public health, Type II errors caused by a regulator's bad judgment, timidity, or anxiety seldom gain public attention. It may be only the employees of the company that makes the product and a few stock market analysts and investors who are likely to be aware of them. Likewise, if a regulator's mistake precipitates a corporate decision to abandon a product, the cause and effect are seldom connected in the public mind. The companies themselves are loath to complain publicly about FDA misjudgments, because the agency wields so much discretionary control over their ability to test and market products. As a consequence, there may be little direct evidence or data to document the lost societal benefits or the culpability of regulatory officials.

Henry I. Miller and Gregory P. Conko,
The Frankenfood Myth: How Protest and
Politics Threaten the Biotech Revolution, *2004.*

disease could be given provisional approval before the completion of final-stage clinical trials and review of the resulting data, as is the FDA's customary process.

Revealing Little

Despite these reforms, the FDA still lacks a transparent mechanism for quantifying the gains in patients' health that are likely to result from faster approvals, for measuring the offsetting costs of potential side effects, and for comparing the two and deciding on that basis whether and to what extent the regulatory process should be streamlined. Put another way, a complete view of the drug-development process would account not only for drug companies' direct costs but for the benefits that producers and consumers are deprived of. . . .

It bears noting that the benefits of an exhaustive review process are far less extensive than is generally supposed. Even especially large, lengthy, and expensive clinical trials will involve only a small fraction of the numbers of patients who will ultimately ingest an approved drug. And the trial cohort may be younger, healthier, or in other ways markedly different from those members of the public at large who take the drugs in question on doctor's orders. Also, doctors may prescribe these drugs for ailments other than the ones for which they were invented and evaluated, further complicating the question of how effective trials are in exposing side effects that the public will be asked to tolerate.

In short, premarket testing may reveal relatively little about a product's safety and efficacy for the potential millions of nonparticipants in trials who ultimately try it. Because the problems associated with many drugs, such as Vioxx, an anti-inflammatory linked to cardiovascular incidents, are subtler than, say, those caused by thalidomide, a new set of tools (including a more intensive system of post-market surveillance) may be better than premarket testing at promoting safety, while permitting effective drugs to reach more quickly all those who might benefit from them.

It goes without saying that innovations such as biomarkers and sophisticated statistical analysis, which might discover a broad range of effects at earlier stages of clinical trials, which wouldn't therefore need to be as large or as extended, should be developed and implemented. Biomarkers are by-products of disease processes (such as decreased numbers of CD4 cells in AIDS cases) or indicators of disease risk (such as cholesterol levels for heart disease) that allow researchers to predict the likelihood of success of treatments without having to wait for the completion of full clinical trials.

Under enhanced post-market surveillance, rapid feedback mechanisms would be in place through which medical practitioners and patients could report on the benefits and side effects of the new treatments they either administer or undergo. In the case of severe rheumatoid arthritis, for example, the FDA would then be in a position to balance the added cardiovascular risks posed by COX-2 [cyclooxygenase-2, an enzyme that causes inflammation] inhibitors against the pain relief that such drugs offer sufferers.

On the basis of evidence that acceleration of the drug-development and approval process does, in fact, offer substantial benefits to patients, we conclude that the FDA should take steps to speed drug development that do not pose an undue hazard to public health and safety.

The Value of Speedier Review

Here we summarize more elaborate recent research that explicitly quantifies the social benefits of a streamlined approval process in the case of three treatments: HAART, for HIV/AIDS; rituximab (Rituxan), for non-Hodgkin's lymphoma; and trastuzumab (Herceptin), for breast cancer.

Our main empirical finding is that the social costs of delays in drug development, as measured by changes in consumer surplus and profits, far outweigh the traditional measure of R&D [research and development] costs discussed above. The analysis applies to a greater number of drugs than the three studied, but we chose those three because they highlight the dramatic impact that new pharmaceuticals can have on well-known, serious, and even fatal diseases, and therefore what the social returns of a faster approval process for these medicines could have been.

We recognize that many otherwise effective drugs do not produce treatment effects that are as large. However, reduced delays in public access to drugs embodying incremental innovations are also likely to generate a very large consumer sur-

plus if they treat large patient populations or introduce therapeutic options to physicians and patients that had not been
previously available. Even new drugs that are not curative may
offer very significant benefits if they improve sufferers' pro-
ductivity (in the form of lower absenteeism, for instance) by
alleviating disabling symptoms.

Our results for the three drugs we reviewed show the following:

- *The sale of these drugs benefited patients far more than
  they did the pharmaceutical firms that developed them.*
  We estimate that HAART was worth $330 billion to
  AIDS patients; rituximab, $8 billion to lymphoma pa-
  tients; and trastuzumab, $137 billion to patients with
  breast cancer. Profits to firms were small in comparison: $27 billion for HAART, $3 billion for rituximab,
  and $9 billion for trastuzumab.

- *A development process that allowed these three drugs to
  enter the market one year earlier would have provided
  enormous social benefits, particularly to patients.* Earlier
  entry by one year would have increased the benefit of
  HAART to patients by $19 billion (a 6 percent
  increase); $310 million in the case of rituximab (4
  percent); and $8 billion in the case of trastuzumab (6
  percent). Profits of the firm marketing HAART would
  have increased by $4 billion (14 percent); $260 million
  for the firm marketing rituximab (8 percent); and $730
  million for the firm marketing trastuzumab. (8
  percent).

- *A process that accelerated entry of these drugs by three
  years would have had even more dramatic effects,* raising
  the benefit by $53 billion (16 percent) for patients who
  took HAART; $850 million (11 percent) for those who
  took rituximab; and $22 billion (15 percent) for those
  who took trastuzumab. Profits from HAART would

have increased by $12 billion (44 percent); $750 million (24 percent) from rituximab; and $2 billion (23 percent) from trastuzumab.

- *A streamlined process would have comparatively little effect on firms' R&D costs.* We find that a reduction in the amount of time a drug spends in Phase III clinical trials or awaiting FDA approval would affect average R&D costs of all drugs by, at most, $40 million each.

Overall, our results suggest that in the case of these three drugs, a streamlined approval process would have generated significant social returns, particularly for patients, and that current measures of the R&D implications of drug lags are misleading. Thus, efforts to streamline the drug-development process that minimize any reduction in safety should be of great social value.

Although it is beyond the scope of this paper to elaborate on specific reforms that could be tried, we would suggest that policymakers consider additional research into and evaluation of the following:

- Speeding recruitment into clinical trials, by, for example, allowing stipends to be paid to volunteer participants. On ethical grounds, such payments are not now permitted. Since forms of permissible employment—for example, construction work—do pose safety hazards, it is not clear why clinical trials in which participants are informed of the risks should merit special treatment, especially in view of the benefits that such participation could bring to the public at large.

- Adopting technologies such as biomarkers that might allow clinical trials to be conducted more expeditiously.

- Continuing to streamline the clinical-trial review process, by, for example, offering FDA regulators performance incentives under the Prescription Drug User Fee

Act to adopt techniques that could more rapidly identify promising new treatments or to evaluate new clinical-trial guidelines. Additional funding could also be used to expand the number of reviewers.

- Establishing an ombudsman [a trusted intermediary] to review the impact of FDA regulations and practices on drug-development times. As explained above, the FDA's natural inclination is to be overly cautious in approving drugs for public distribution. An ombudsman could restrain this tendency.

- Establishing permanent funding of the Reagan-Udall Foundation. Created but not funded by PDUFA's 2007 reauthorization, the foundation is charged with modernizing the drug-development process in consultation with the FDA.

"A [behind-the-counter] class [of drugs] would expand the range of conditions that patients can self-treat without spending time or money on a doctor's visit."

The FDA Should Allow Pharmacists to Dispense Behind-the-Counter Drugs

Rebecca Burkholder

Rebecca Burkholder is vice president of health policy for the National Consumers League and a former health care attorney. In the following viewpoint, Burkholder supports a new classification of drugs available without a prescription called behind-the-counter (BTC) drugs, to increase access to medications and lower medical costs. Intended for self-diagnosis and self-treatment, BTC drugs must be dispensed by a pharmacist, she claims, to consult with the consumer on the safe and effective use of the medication, recognize symptoms that indicate a more serious condition, and ensure against the risk of drug interactions and inappropriate dosing.

As you read, consider the following questions:

1. How would the loss of insurance coverage of drugs classified as BTC affect consumers with insurance, as stated by Burkholder?

2. In the author's view, how may privacy issues impact access to BTC drugs?

3. How can pharmacists protect consumers from drug interactions and double dosing with BTC medications, according to Burkholder?

The National Consumers League (NCL) is a private, non-profit advocacy group representing consumers on marketplace and workplace issues. We are pleased to be able to comment today on the concept of behind the counter (or BTC) availability of drugs. For years NCL has been in favor of a third class of drugs, where certain drugs would be placed behind the pharmacy counter and only available with the intervention of a pharmacist. NCL believes that this class of drugs could improve access for patients, but we have numerous concerns about how such a system will work safely and effectively. . . .

A New Class of Drugs

Should there be BTC availability of certain drug products and why?

Historically NCL has been in favor of a BTC drug class to increase patient access to those medications they can safely use, after consultation with a pharmacist, to self-treat conditions they can self-diagnose. Consumers today are taking a more active role in their health care and self-diagnosing and self-medicating with over the counter [OTC] medications, as well as dietary supplements and herbals. A BTC class would expand the range of conditions that patients can self-treat without spending time or money on a doctor's visit. Quality pharmacy consultation would be critical to ensuring that the appropriate medication is selected and taken safely and effectively. While a BTC class would appear to benefit consumers by giving them greater access, questions remain—such as, which drugs should be in this class? How will pharmacists counsel patients? Because of the many questions regarding how a BTC class system would work, we support the suggestion put forth by Consumers Union that FDA [Food and Drug Administration] should first test the BTC concept in a couple of states.

Patient Access to Medications

How will BTC impact patient access and cost?

A BTC class would likely increase access to medications for consumers since they would not have to obtain a doctor's prescription for the medication. For the 47 million consumers without health insurance, a BTC class would increase their options for self-treatment without the added expense of a doctor's visit. We also need to remember that underserved and rural communities do not always have access to a pharmacy, and thus [would have] less access to BTC drugs.

Regarding the cost of BTC drugs, for consumers with insurance, a drug switched from prescription to BTC could mean the loss of insurance coverage for that drug. Thus, there may be additional costs for these consumers, if they now must pay the entire cost of the drug. But the consumer would also save the cost of a doctor's visit, the co-pay for the medication, and the time spent in the waiting room. To ensure that costs are not shifted to the consumer, we suggest that when a drug moves from prescription to BTC, the insurance coverage stays the same.

Concerns about privacy regarding medications may also impact access because most pharmacies do not have private places to talk to the pharmacist. Some patients may not feel comfortable receiving counseling from a pharmacist for a BTC

A Benefit to the Public

Medications selected for BTC status must provide a benefit to the public. Many individuals, especially those without health insurance, may not have a primary care physician and thus no ready access to prescription medications. Making certain drugs available BTC would provide access to treatment regimens that those patients might not otherwise obtain.

Academy of Managed Care Pharmacy,
June 2009. http://amcp.org.

medication, such as oral contraception. If counseling is required, some patients may forgo the treatment due to embarrassment or feeling uncomfortable receiving counseling in a non-private area from a pharmacist they do not know. For other consumers access would increase since it will be easier for them to purchase oral contraception at a local drug store, without the expense and hassle of a doctor's visit. Establishment of a truly private pharmacy counseling area should be required for a BTC class to ensure that access would increase, and not decrease.

The Pharmacist's Role

What is the role of the pharmacist?

Clearly, the role of the pharmacist is critical to ensuring the safe and effective use of BTC drugs. We know that consumers do NOT always read the labels of OTC products they purchase, and over a quarter have trouble reading and understanding the label. Thus, the pharmacist should be available to provide one-on-one private counseling, to ensure consumers understand the appropriate use of BTC medications.

However, pharmacists are not always available for counseling, or the line at the pharmacy counter is too long, and time short. And many times consumers sign away their right to counseling, without even knowing what they are signing. We know from experiences in other countries with a BTC or pharmacy class of drugs that counseling is not always engaged in or complete. A 2004 study of Australian pharmacy counseling found that the majority of time the advice given was "poor" and questions were not asked to ensure that the medication discussed was appropriate. Also of note was that often the first contact for the consumer was the pharmacy assistant, not the actual pharmacist. In a 2002 study of New Zealand pharmacies, consumers often found it difficult to distinguish between the pharmacist and assistant staff. Consumers were able to confirm that a pharmacist was definitely involved in counseling in only 46% of visits. And no counseling was given at all for 10% of the consumers obtaining an anti-fungal medication (which required pharmacy intervention).

In the United States, pharmacists continue to be a trusted source for consumers, and in some neighborhoods more accessible than a primary care physician, but they need to come out from behind the counter. A pharmacist's role includes assisting consumers who have trouble reading English or need extra help to understand the drugs they are taking.

When self-medicating, consumers need assistance with diagnosing because they may not recognize the symptoms of a more serious condition and delay a necessary visit to the doctor. For example, stomach pain—gastrointestinal distress—can be a symptom of a number of medical problems. While consumers may use a proton pump inhibitor, such as Prilosec, for symptomatic relief [of acid indigestion], potentially serious GI [gastrointestinal] problems may be missed because a doctor was not consulted. This underlines the need for appropriate pharmacy counseling about when consumers should consult a doctor.

For certain chronic conditions, such as high cholesterol and diabetes, pharmacists should encourage an initial physician evaluation and follow up to assess the progress of the disease. While it may be possible for pharmacists to conduct some follow-up testing (and the logistics of this would need to be worked out), there must be clear pharmacy counseling urging people to check with their physician before use and to continue to have regular visits while taking the medication. A few years ago, with the possible switch of a low-dose statin medication to OTC status, NCL was concerned that consumers would not consult their doctors before or during the use of an OTC statin. Based on a survey we commissioned, consumers overwhelmingly demonstrated their willingness to continue to consult with their doctors. If FDA determines low-dose statins are appropriate for a BTC class, how would pharmacists be able to ensure that patients visited their physician? Would a consumer need to document that they saw a physician before a pharmacist dispensed a BTC drug?

A pharmacist's role would also include providing continuing education on safe and effective use of BTC medications. Even though a drug may be in a BTC class for years and consumers who have been counseled may need less assistance, the consumer who just begins therapy will need active pharmacy counseling. Because consumers often mistakenly believe that more is better, particularly with medications that do not require a prescription, pharmacists will need to continue to check for appropriate dosage. And, pharmacists will also need to pay special attention to the risk of interactions between BTC drugs and other prescriptions, OTCs, and dietary supplements. A pharmacist should have access to the patient's full medication list to avoid interactions and double dosing. Since many consumers [order] their medications by mail or by Internet, it would be the responsibility of the consumer to maintain an up to date medication record to share with their pharmacist. Ideally, an integrated E[lectronic]-prescribing system is needed for a BTC class to be safe and not result in more confusion among multiple prescribers in multiple settings.

Availability Status

Should BTC availability be a temporary status or a permanent status?

While a transition class may be appropriate for some medications in order to determine if they can be used safely and effectively as OTCs, for other medications a permanent BTC class may be more appropriate. This would depend on the safety profile of the drug, including potential for side effects and harmful interactions.

Regarding how FDA determines which drugs are moved into a BTC class, we suggest, as Consumers Union does, that rather than respond to random petitions to move a drug to a BTC status, that FDA convene an advisory committee once a year to consider several drugs FDA staff believes are good candidates for BTC.

The issue of whether BTC is a permanent or temporary status raises the question of how the drug is regulated regarding advertising—can the drug be advertised to consumers as an OTC, or as a prescription drug (and therefore required to include a summary of risks and benefits)? How a drug is advertised will impact consumer perception of its risks and benefits, and subsequent use of the medication.

Ensuring Patient Safety

What measures would be necessary to ensure patient safety?

1) Establishment of a system that ensures quality pharmacy counseling occurs, which would require more than just the consumer's signature. The consumer could be asked to check off and certify that they received counseling in specific areas (such as interactions).

2) Certain information should be conveyed to consumers through counseling, labeling and any promotional materials. This includes:

—when a doctor should be consulted.

—common interactions, AND

—a 1-800 number and website for consumers to contact if they have any questions, along with MedWatch contact information to report adverse events.

Lastly, before a drug moves to BTC status, drug manufacturers should be required to conduct a public education campaign for consumers, as well as prescribers and pharmacists, to explain that the drug will be available BTC, that a pharmacist must be consulted to obtain the medication, and any potential risks.

> *"This notion of a third class of drugs has been tried, and there is much evidence that it did not work."*

The FDA Should Not Allow Pharmacists to Dispense Behind-the-Counter Drugs

Sidney M. Wolfe

In the following viewpoint, Sidney M. Wolfe opposes the classification of behind-the-counter (BTC) drugs, which are dispensed by a consulting pharmacist without a prescription. Drawing from studies, Wolfe states that the countries using the system have not increased access to medications or produced significant cost savings. Furthermore, the consultations with pharmacists are often incomplete or not universally given, he contends, and do not gather information on symptoms and other medications. Ultimately, BTC drug classification removes the role of a doctor, potentially harming the public, the author maintains. Wolfe is the director of Public Citizen's Health Research Group, editor of WorstPills.org, and an adjunct professor at Case Western Reserve University School of Medicine.

As you read, consider the following questions:

1. What figures does Wolfe provide that BTC drug classification does not increase access to medications?

2. Why do drug companies favor BTC drug classification, in the author's opinion?

3. What example does Wolfe give in his support of the switch of prescription drugs to over-the-counter status?

When the Food and Drug Administration (FDA) makes an important policy decision, the evidence for the benefits and risks of that decision needs to be weighed as carefully as the evidence concerning the benefit/risk balance of a drug. In the case of behind-the-counter availability of drugs, it is useful to hear the opinions of various parties, including those with obvious financial conflicts of interest whose opinions can be predicted. But before any decision is reached there needs to be evidence that benefits outweigh the risks of such a new system, particularly because new legislation would probably be needed if behind-the-counter availability of drugs is to be established as a general principle. The necessary evidence does not currently exist, as I will discuss later.

Thirty-three years ago [in 1974], spurred in part by pharmacists' desires to restrict certain over-the-counter (OTC) drugs to pharmacist-only or behind-the-counter availability, the FDA stated that "There is at this time no public health concern that would justify the creation of a third class of drugs to be dispensed only by a pharmacist or in a pharmacy. The 'third class of drug' issue is at this time solely an economic issue. The Commissioner therefore categorically rejects the establishment of a third class of drugs at this time".

Value Yet to Be Demonstrated

More recently, in 1994, Congressman John Dingell asked the Government Accountability Office (GAO) to do a comprehensive study to collect data on the experiences of other countries that had, by then, implemented such systems. Congressman Dingell's request was prompted in part by the wishes of some individuals in Congress to revive the idea of behind-the-counter availability for certain drugs. The study involved 10 countries: Canada, Australia and eight European countries. It was made public in August, 1995, and was entitled "NON-PRESCRIPTION DRUGS—Value of a Pharmacist-Controlled Class Has Yet to Be Demonstrated."

I will quote from the findings of this study, which is the last comprehensive review of this topic to be done.

The results in brief were:

Little evidence supports the establishment of a pharmacy or pharmacist class of drugs in the United States at this time, as either a fixed or a transition class. The evidence that is available tends to undermine the contention that major benefits are being obtained in the countries that have such a class. This conclusion is substantiated by six points. (1) Reliable and valid studies that examine the effect of different drug distribution systems on overall health and health care system costs do not exist. (2) While a pharmacy or pharmacist class exists in all 10 countries, it is not used with any frequency in any of them to facilitate the movement of drugs to sale outside specialized drug outlets. (3) The European Union has decided not to impose any particular drug distribution system on its member countries because it has found no evidence of the superiority of one system over another. (4) There is no clear pattern of increased or decreased access to drugs as nonprescription products where a pharmacist or pharmacy class exists. (5) While a pharmacy or pharmacist class is assumed by some to improve safeguards against drug misuse and abuse, in the 10 countries these safeguards are easily circumvented, and studies show that pharmacist counseling is infrequent and incomplete. (6) Experience in Florida with a class of drugs similar to a pharmacist class has not been successful; pharmacists have not regularly prescribed these drugs, and recordkeeping requirements have not been followed.

Cost

The body of the GAO report elaborated on some of these points:

> Our interviews with officials in the study countries indicated that the cost savings from fewer physicians' visits may not be as great as expected. They said that many patients do not pay the full price for a prescribed drug. For instance, an insured patient might have only a $5.00 copayment for a prescription drug while having to pay the full price for a nonprescription product. Patients might thus have an incentive to go to doctors for a prescription.
>
> The results of the studies in the United States are rather similar to those in countries where the sale of at least some nonprescription drugs is restricted to pharmacies. *In general, the theory of pharmacy practice diverges from the reality* (emphasis added). The advice of pharmacists is often appropriate but not universally given. In addition, it is often incomplete, with little information being given to customers on such items as possible side effects. In other words, what information is given is accurate, but not enough was passed on to consumers. Researchers consistently found a lack of information-gathering on the part of pharmacists. For instance, information is often not gathered on symptoms and other medications.

Pharmacists Cannot Counsel Patients

The theory that pharmacists can counsel patients on OTC, prescription or behind-the-counter drugs diverges from the reality, as stated by the GAO. Evaluation of this includes the 1990 OBRA [Omnibus Budget Reconciliation Act] law requiring a system of pharmacist information for patients for prescription drugs that has not worked nearly as well as hoped and the above-mentioned pharmacist counseling for OTC and behind-the-counter drugs.

Doctors' Roles Replaced

More recently, there are some evaluations—surveys of pharmacists—of the 2004 UK decision to make the statin drug simvastatin available in a pharmacist-only setting without requiring a doctor's prescription. Some of the findings of two published studies on this topic are as follows:

Questionnaires were returned by 1,156 community pharmacists (57.8%). Nine hundred and fifty-six respondents (82.7%) reported no sales of simvastatin in the previous fourteen days. Eighty-two (7.1%) sold one pack, 40 (3.5%) sold two.

Health promotion material aimed at reducing cardiovascular risk was displayed to customers in just over half of the pharmacies (602, 52.1%).

> This is the first relatively large-scale national study to report community pharmacists' experiences of OTC simvastatin in Great Britain. The majority of respondents had undertaken an array of continuing education, had established sales protocols and expressed confidence in making an appropriate cardiovascular risk assessment in line with the OTC license. Most considered this to be an area requiring personal input from the pharmacist rather than being delegated to other pharmacy staff. However, very few sales had actually taken place during the study period. . . . [Thus] major concerns relating to the need for full cardiovascular risk assessment, access to full clinical information prior to simvastatin use and the lack of an evidence base for the licensed dose reflect reservations voiced by the medical profession.

This notion of a third class of drugs has been tried, and there is much evidence that it did not work. A doctor writes a prescription, a pharmacist fills it. If the doctor is removed from the equation, the public could be harmed, as evidenced by the concerns of UK pharmacists about simvastatin.

The positions taken by those involved are very predictable. Pharmacists support it, but doctors oppose it because their roles are replaced. Some drug companies like it because they see it as a way to boost sales (as in the case of the third try to switch a statin to this category). Companies who sell to 7–11s and other markets . . . don't like it because many of their outlets don't have a pharmacist so they can't sell third-class drugs.

Pharmacists are well-skilled and often know a lot about the drugs they dispense. But in practice, they often do not counsel when asked to because they do not have the time. There is no mechanism to reimburse them for their time. As a policy it wouldn't work. It would probably take a Congressional law to make it happen.

Twenty years ago, the painkillers ibuprofen and naproxen were only available by prescription. As we learned more about the drugs and their safety, those drugs became available over the counter. Pain is an easy self-diagnosis. Thus far, the prescription-to-OTC switch process has worked quite well.

The current push for a behind-the-counter class was precipitated by drug companies who make statins and want to switch them to OTC. I have testified twice already and I'm going to testify next month for a third time opposing statins becoming OTC.

I am also concerned about the privacy issue. Even with prescription drugs, there have been pharmacists who have sold information regarding doctors' prescribing practices although there is, as of yet, no evidence that patient confidentiality has been compromised. In order to protect patients, there would have to be some safeguards built in to extend to the patient-pharmacist relationship the confidentiality that people now have with their doctors.

Periodical and Internet Sources Bibliography

The following articles have been selected to supplement the diverse views presented in this chapter.

Ellie Dolgin	"When It Takes Two to Tango, FDA Suggests a New Regulatory Dance," *Nature Medicine*, March 2011.
William Faloon	"FDA Delay of One Drug Causes 82,000 Lost Life-Years," *Life Extension Magazine*, November 2010.
Scott Gavura	"Rx, OTC, BTC—Wading into Pharmacy's Alphabet Soup," Science-Based Medicine, May 13, 2010. www.sciencebasedmedicine.org.
John Gever	"FDA Faulted for Spotty Oversight of Data Coming from Overseas," ABC News, June 24, 2010. http://abcnews.go.com.
Gardiner Harris	"What's Behind an F.D.A. Stamp?," *New York Times*, September 29, 2008.
Daniel Healy	"Plan BTC: The Case for a Third Class of Drugs in the United States," *Food and Drug Law Journal*, vol. 63, no. 1, 2008.
Peter D. Jacobson and Wendy E. Parmet	"A New Era of Unapproved Drugs: The Case of *Abigail Alliance v. Von Eschenbach*," *Journal of the American Medical Association*, January 10, 2007.
Randall S. Safford	"Regulating Off-Label Drug Use—Rethinking the Role of the FDA," *New England Journal of Medicine*, April 3, 2008.
Carl E. Schneider	"Constitutional Flaw?," *Hastings Center Report*, July–August 2009.
Melissa Sherer	"BTC Drugs: Is There a Pharmacist Available?," *ComputerTalk*, January/February 2008.

OPPOSING
VIEWPOINTS®
SERIES

CHAPTER 3

Are Pharmaceutical Marketing Practices Adequately Regulated?

Chapter Preface

In 1997, the Food and Drug Administration (FDA) adjusted its guidelines to allow pharmaceutical companies to advertise prescription drugs on television. It relaxed the requirement that all risk information and precautions must be summarized in the ad—including potential side effects, interactions with other drugs, and warnings to individuals with certain conditions—to just the major and most common ones. Known as direct-to-consumer (DTC) advertising, this practice is forbidden in every other country except New Zealand.

The administration classifies three types of DTC advertising. "Product claim" ads state the drug's name, illness or condition treated, and its benefits and risks. "Reminder" ads state the drug's name, but not its uses. "Help-seeking" ads describe an illness or condition, but do not state the drug's name. Only product claim ads must disclose the major risks and precautions and communicate to viewers how or where to get the complete information, such as a consultation with a physician, toll-free phone number, website address, or print ad published in a current magazine issue.

Product claim ads can violate regulations in several ways. The ad can only suggest uses of a drug that are approved by the FDA. In addition, information about a drug's benefits and risks must be in fair balance. "This does not mean that equal space must be given to risks and benefits in print ads, or equal time to risks and benefits in broadcast ads," the administration explains. "The amount of time or space needed to present risk information will depend on the drug's risks and the way that both the benefits and risks are presented,"[1] the agency adds. And therapeutic claims must be supported by re-

1. Food and Drug Administration, "Drug Advertising: A Glossary of Terms," June 24, 2009. www.fda.gov/Drugs/ResourcesForYou/Consumers/PrescriptionDrugAdvertising/ucm072025.htm.

liable studies and not misleading. "If FDA determines that claims are not supported, it will take action to have the ad fixed,"[2] it states. In the following chapter, the authors discuss whether DTC advertising and other marketing tactics of pharmaceutical companies are adequately regulated.

2. Food and Drug Administration, "Incorrect Product Claim Ad," June 24, 2009. www.fda.gov/Drugs/ResourcesForYou/Consumers/PrescriptionDrugAdvertising/ ucm082282.htm.

> *"Over the past several years, prescription drug companies have been required to report to various state agencies the promotional expenses incurred in their interactions with healthcare practitioners."*

Pharmaceutical Marketing Practices Are Strictly Regulated

John Patrick Oroho, Christine N. Bradshaw, and Christopher R. Corallo

In the following viewpoint, John Patrick Oroho, Christine N. Bradshaw, and Christopher R. Corallo contend that the marketing activities of pharmaceutical companies are actively regulated. They maintain that sales representatives face restrictions in accessing medical institutions and giving health care practitioners gifts and meals; in many instances, representatives must also comply with lobbyist registration and disclosure requirements and lobbyist laws when engaging with government employees. For pharmaceutical detailers, licensure and ethical marketing practices may be enforced, the authors claim. Oroho is a princi-

John Patrick Oroho, Christine N. Bradshaw, and Christopher R. Corallo, "Sales Rep Nightmares: Emerging Issues in Marketing Compliance," *Update*, vol. 3, May/June 2009, pp. 40–45.

pal at the law firm Porzio, Bromberg & Newman in Morristown, New Jersey, where Bradshaw is an associate. Corallo is a compliance audit associate at Bioment in Parsippany, New Jersey.

As you read, consider the following questions:

1. What do medical schools and university hospitals require of sales representatives or vendors, as described by the authors?

2. What may be considered unacceptable gifts by institutions, according to Oroho, Bradshaw, and Corallo?

3. What interactions are prohibited for pharmaceutical detailers in the District of Columbia's code of ethics, as stated by the authors?

Over the past several years, prescription drug companies have been required to report to various state agencies the promotional expenses incurred in their interactions with healthcare practitioners (HCPs). Medical device companies are increasingly subject to these state disclosure laws as well. Currently, the federal government is also considering legislation that would require both pharmaceutical and medical device manufacturers to disclose "the value, nature and purpose" of promotional expenditures directed toward HCPs.

Many state-regulated interactions with HCPs involve sales representatives, detailers or other company representatives operating in the field and engaged in promotional activities. The regulatory environment for promotional interactions has become quite volatile and states, as well as individual institutions, are calling for more transparency and accountability. Given pending federal legislation and recent changes to the Pharmaceutical Research and Manufacturers of America's (PhRMA's) *Code on Interactions with Healthcare Professionals* and the Advanced Medical Technology Association's (AdvaMed's) *Code of Ethics on Interactions with Health*

Care Professionals, sales representative training on and awareness of these issues are critical to a company's efforts to ensure compliance with marketing-related laws and guidelines.

This article focuses on three types of restrictions that go beyond state marketing disclosures: medical school and institutional restrictions on the interactions between sales representatives and HCPs; state or institutional classification of sales representatives as lobbyists under the state or local government's lobbying laws; and the sales representative licensure law recently enacted in the District of Columbia, which requires that company representatives become licensed before interacting with HCPs.

Medical Schools and Institutions

Many medical institutions, including medical schools and university hospitals, require sales representatives or vendors to register with the institution, make an appointment with specific HCPs, obtain identification badges upon arrival at the facility, and agree to comply with institution policies and procedures prior to gaining access to grounds and staff. A sales representative's access also may be limited to only non-patient areas, unless the institution determines that the sales representative should provide in-service training on devices or other equipment.

Some institutions impose additional procedural requirements. For example, the University of Michigan Health System requires registrants to sign a statement certifying that he or she has received, reviewed and agrees to comply with all policies and guidelines provided by the institution. New Jersey's Hunterdon Healthcare System requires vendors to disclose any conflicts of interest. Other medical institutions, such as the Duke University Health System, require registrants to sign a confidentiality agreement as part of their registration process.

Additionally, many medical institutions require payment of registration fees by either each registering representative or the vendor itself. The University of Illinois Medical Center at Chicago requires registering representatives to pay a $250 fee annually. The Hunterdon Healthcare System requires both representatives and the company to register with the institution, and the company/vendor must pay a fee ranging from $25 to $250, depending on the extent of the vendor's business relationship with Hunterdon.

Institutions around the country are adopting policies regarding a company representative's ability to provide meals or gifts to HCPs, medical staff, students and other personnel that, in some cases, are more restrictive than state law and industry guidances. As such, it is necessary for companies to take notice of a particular medical institution's definition of the term "gift." Most institutions' policies identify a range of items that may fall under the definition of an unacceptable gift, including all or some of the following: food, pens, pads, mugs, textbooks, office supplies, cash, entertainment, payment for travel, and time and participation associated with continuing medical education events. . . .

Lobbyist Registration

Beyond limiting physical access to their faculties, some medical schools and institutions may require sales or vendor representatives to register and comply with state or local government lobbyist registration requirements. In Florida's Miami-Dade County, the Jackson Health System (JHS) has a policy that requires, among other things, that:

> all Vendor Representatives, prior to engaging in any conversation or communication, verbal or written, with a County/JHS Employee or JHS Medical Staff Member for the purpose of selling, marketing or influencing a decision to purchase any product or service that shall require the expenditure of County/JHS funds, must first become "registered" with the County as a "lobbyist."

In December 2006, the Miami-Dade County Commission on Ethics and Public Trust issued an advisory opinion that concluded that "seeking to influence the action, recommendation or decision of County personnel" triggers the lobbyist registration requirement because University of Miami physicians "are functioning as County personnel when they make decisions regarding particular products and services for use in Jackson facilities."

Thus, not only do sales representatives need to register as lobbyists when interacting with HCPs at JHS facilities, they also will be considered lobbyists and must register with Miami-Dade County whenever they interact with any HCP who works with JHS, even if only on a part-time or temporary basis.

State Lobbying Laws

Most states have lobbying laws that regulate interactions between government employees and industry representatives. "Government employees" is often a broadly defined term, and may include public servants, public officials, committee members or other members of administrative bodies. While sales representatives' actions generally fall outside the scope of most states' lobbyist laws, at least one state has made clear that its law applies to sales representatives' interactions with certain HCPs.

In Louisiana, lobbying of executive branch employees occurs when industry seeks to influence "any act by an executive branch agency or official to effectuate the public powers, functions and duties of an executive branch official or an executive branch agency, including but not limited to any act in the nature of policymaking, rulemaking, adjudication, licensing, regulation or enforcement." . . .

Pharmaceutical Detailer Licensure

Pharmaceutical companies, contract sales organizations and related entities have their own standards and requirements

"I believe I have a new approach to psychotherapy, but, like everything else, the FDA tells me it first has to be tested on mice."

"I believe I have a new approach to psychotherapy, but, like everything else, the FDA tells me it first has to be tested on mice," cartoon by S. Harris, www.CartoonStock.com. Copyright © S. Harris. Reproduction rights obtainable from www.CartoonStock.com.

that dictate the qualification requirements a person must satisfy to effectively perform promotional activities on its behalf. The District of Columbia has now entered into the arena of establishing qualifications for sales representatives by passing first-of-its-kind legislation in February 2008.

Under the District of Columbia law, pharmaceutical sales representatives who are hired to sell, market or promote their company's product to a HCP in the District must be licensed as a "pharmaceutical detailer." In June 2008, the District of Columbia's Department of Health approved regulations that require pharmaceutical detailers to be licensed beginning April 1, 2009.

Amended regulations were adopted and finalized in April 2009. The revised regulations clarify that the "practice of pharmaceutical detailing" means representing a pharmaceutical manufacturer or labeler and communicating, in person, with a licensed HCP or his or her employee or representative in D.C. in a non-conference setting for the purpose of selling, marketing or promoting a prescription or OTC [over-the-counter] drug for use in humans, or providing information to sell, market or promote the drug.

Sales representatives who seek to detail in the District must complete a New License Application, which requires representatives to provide, among other things:

- Proof of graduation from an institution of higher learning (note that this education requirement may be waived if the sales representative can show proof of full-time employment as a pharmaceutical detailer for a 12-month period);

- Social Security Number;

- Passport photo;

- Drivers License;

- Notarized "Affidavit to Abide by Code of Ethics"; and

- License fee of $175.

Once the sales representative is licensed, he or she must complete at least 15 hours of continuing education credits approved by the Board of Pharmacy over the two-year licensure term.

The District of Columbia Code of Ethics specifies prohibited interactions, including but not limited to:

- Deceptive or misleading marketing;

- Using a misleading title or designation;

- Attending patient examinations without written patient consent;

- Willfully harassing or intimidating HCPs;

- Making sales calls to a HCP who has requested to no longer receive such calls; and

- Offering a gift or remuneration of any kind to a member of a medication advisory committee.

In addition, the Code of Ethics affirmatively requires the detailer to:

- Provide information to HCPs that is accurate and fairly balanced in compliance with FDA policies and practices for providing information to HCPs; and

- Comply with the standards established by the PhRMA Code.

There are many components to the detailer law that were created to monitor the activity of detailers. One noteworthy element is the Board of Pharmacy's authority "to collect information from licensed pharmaceutical detailers relating to their communications with licensed health professionals, or with employees or representatives of licensed health professionals, located in the District." Consequently, sales representatives must maintain detailed records of communications and documentation referenced or discussed during the promotional meeting between the pharmaceutical detailer and the HCP. . . .

Effective lines of communication are critical in today's compliance landscape. Sales Operations and Compliance departments must work together to assess existing and emergent limitations on sales representative site access, gift and meal restrictions, lobbyist registration and reporting requirements, and detailer licensure obligations. In addition, compliance professionals must ensure that their sales personnel understand the true importance of recording and reporting promotional expenses. The move by the federal government to adopt disclosure legislation may further complicate internal business decisions regarding expense capture, unless a unified industry approach is adopted. In the interim, annual process and data audits, employee training, timely revisions to policies and procedures, and effective state law monitoring systems are key to maintaining successful sales force compliance strategies.

"The FDA has vowed to crack down on increasingly aggressive marketing tactics ... but ... the agency lacks the resources to sharply curtail misleading drug ads."

Aggressive Pharmaceutical Marketing Practices Often Outpace Regulatory Efforts

Susan Heavey and Lisa Richwine

In the following viewpoint, Susan Heavey and Lisa Richwine contend that the marketing practices of the pharmaceutical industry outpace the oversight of the Food and Drug Administration (FDA). From using social networking sites to holding social events, drug companies are looking to new, creative methods to sell their products and reach consumers, Heavey and Richwine state. However, the FDA has not yet established regulatory guidelines for online marketing, the authors add, and is struggling to monitor the flood of television and promotional campaigns for misrepresentations of the risks or benefits of drugs. Based in Washington, D.C., Heavey is a health reporter for Reuters news service, and Richwine is a Reuters journalist.

As you read, consider the following questions:

1. What statements were made at a brunch about Mirena, a birth control device, as stated by the authors?

2. According to Heavey and Richwine, how many pharmaceutical ads must be monitored each year by how many FDA staff members?

3. What does Bayer Healthcare say about the FDA's social media policies, as cited by the authors?

(Reuters—It wasn't what you would call a casual get-together.

In February 2009, a popular New York blogger attended a brunch with fellow "frazzled moms." They took in tips from a style expert and listened to a nurse extol the virtues of Mirena, a birth control device sold by Bayer Healthcare.

The nurse was on Bayer's payroll. In a series of events organized with the help of a women's website, Mom Central, the pharmaceutical company gathered a captive audience of young mothers. It provided the nurse with a script and had the women fill out a survey before they left.

The sessions earned a stern rebuke from the U.S. Food and Drug Administration. In a letter to Bayer Healthcare made public earlier this year, the agency faulted the drugmaker for telling "busy moms" that using its intrauterine device (IUD) "will result in increased levels of intimacy, romance and, by implication, emotional satisfaction."

Besides hyping the product, the nurse failed to disclose potential risks. "Here you have a company hiring a third-party to invite people into a home like a Tupperware party," said Thomas Abrams, whose department oversees pharmaceutical marketing reviews at the FDA. "That was extremely, extremely concerning to us because this product has risks—risk of infection, loss of fertility. Huge risk."

Under the Obama administration, the FDA has vowed to crack down on increasingly aggressive marketing tactics—both online and off. But even Abrams acknowledges the agency lacks the resources to sharply curtail misleading drug ads.

Downturn or no, the pharmaceutical industry hasn't been skimping on advertising. In 2009, companies spent a vast $4.8 billion to reach out to consumers in the United States—the only country besides New Zealand that allows direct-to-consumer advertising—up from nearly $4.7 billion the year before, according to tracking firm Kantar Media.

To drug companies, it is all part of patient education. But consumer advocates, some lawmakers and others see the barrage of ads as a way to push medicines that people may not need as well as raise the nation's overall healthcare costs.

As media splinters into a sea of Internet blogs, on-demand television and niche publications, companies are racing to keep pace. Websites and digital technology offer powerful tools that make it easier, cheaper and quicker to target specific groups. And drugmakers are relying more on celebrities and other methods to make their products stand out.

For example, last year the FDA warned Abbott Laboratories over a promotional DVD featuring former basketball star and HIV patient Earvin "Magic" Johnson that the agency said suggested the company's HIV drug Kaletra was safer and more effective than proven.

Agency staff have also slapped Allergan Inc. for its website promoting its eyelash-boosting drug Latisse, saying various webpages did not tell potential consumers about possible risks, such as extraneous hair growth if the product touches the skin elsewhere, and downplayed possible allergic reactions.

Earlier this year, Novartis earned a warning for two websites it sponsored—www.gistalliance.com and www.cmlalliance.com—to promote its leukemia drug Gleevec. The FDA

"Most of them are about Viagra," cartoon by Mike Peters. Mike Peters Editorial Cartoon used by permission of Mike Peters and the Cartoonist Group. All rights reserved.

said although the sites never used the therapy's brand name, they clearly alluded to it and yet failed to mention critical side effects.

All told, the number of warnings the agency has sent drugmakers has ballooned, despite voluntary industry guidelines established in 2005 to help curb complaints. In 2008, under the Bush administration, the FDA sent just 21 notices to companies for violating the agency's marketing standards. Last year, it sent 41 letters to companies. Already this year, it is outpacing that effort, having issued 45 warnings through August 28.

Creative Marketing

The FDA's Division of Drug Marketing, Advertising and Communications reviews advertisements and other promotional items before and after they run to try to ensure companies do not mislead consumers or make false claims.

Its job isn't getting any easier. "Companies have become more aggressive with their promotion, more creative," said Abrams, a former pharmaceutical salesman who spent seven years working in sales and marketing for two different companies before moving to the FDA's promotional division for the last 16 years.

The advertising universe has been transformed in other ways since his days pushing promotions in New Jersey, home to several of the nation's top drugmakers.

Facebook, Twitter, YouTube and other social media networks are the new frontier in marketing, and drugmakers are dipping in like everyone else. Pfizer Inc, GlaxoSmithKline Plc, Bristol-Myers Squibb and AstraZeneca all have Twitter feeds, and some also have blogs.

Unlike the case for print and broadcast, the FDA has yet to lay out guidelines for industry to follow, though Abrams said the agency aims to release a draft later this year.

"We are developing separate guidance that are issue-specific and can apply to the various mediums used on the Internet," he told Reuters. For example, the agency will advise companies how to respond when consumers make an unprompted request for information on a drug.

The lack of guidelines remains a sore point for the industry. "FDA has continued enforcement actions without these clear standards," said Jeff Francer, a lawyer at the Pharmaceutical Research and Manufacturers of America (PhRMA), the industry lobby group that made the 2005 pledge to clean up ads.

In comments submitted to the FDA ahead of the expected new guidelines, drugmakers made their feelings known. Officials for diversified healthcare company Johnson & Johnson urged the agency to "keep its approach as simple and flexible as possible," in a letter this past February.

And Big Pharma has acquired some unlikely allies. Internet companies that thrive on online advertisements, including YouTube's parent Google Inc and rival Yahoo! Inc. have joined forces with drugmakers in pressing the FDA for clear standards.

"Running to Keep Up"

Even without the Internet, FDA officials would have trouble keeping up.

Congress has helped deliver a handful more staffers to help tackle the growing flood of ads, but the agency still has just 57 officials charged with reviewing roughly 75,000 marketing items a year, Abrams noted. They review "thousands and thousands" but can't get to them all, he said.

As a result, agency officials say they must prioritize which promotions get checked first. Those that could have the biggest effect on public health top the pile.

To make matters worse, Congress moved to allow industry funds to boost FDA ad reviews but never fully authorized the program. Companies could have voluntarily paid a fee to have the FDA screen their television commercials before they ran, rather than later when they could get a warning.

FDA Commissioner Margaret Hamburg, who took over in May 2009, has said staffers simply can't cope with the volume. "We're sort of always running to keep up," Hamburg, a former New York City health chief and public health expert, told lawmakers at a U.S. House of Representatives appropriations subcommittee in March.

"We do review the ads and can take action when we think there are misrepresentations or inadequate presentation of risks, but the volume makes it very, very difficult," she said. "The fact is: we don't review them, sign off, and then they go up."

Insufficient staff isn't the agency's only problem. It is also hampered by antiquated technology systems.

At a time when digital videos take seconds to upload and can reach millions of views in minutes, the FDA's marketing reviewers read storyboards of television and Internet spots on paper, which are archived in a separate room across the agency's 130-acre campus. As with other government entities, the division is moving toward electronic submissions but isn't there yet.

To ease the workload, the agency recently enlisted doctors to report misleading promotions aimed at medical professionals. Its "Bad Ad" campaign seeks to teach physicians how to spot questionable promotions or statements and then report them to the agency voluntarily.

So far, it has received about 100 complaints through the effort.

Nevertheless, consumer activists say FDA's overall approach is likely to fall short. Abrams' office "certainly needs more money and manpower to be regularly monitoring this kind of stuff," said Steve Findlay, a senior health policy analyst for Consumers Union, an independent non-profit group aimed at protecting buyers.

Findlay said the industry's efforts at self-policing have helped, especially among larger companies, but some companies have clearly crossed the line. "We're still seeing drug ads that are not completely balanced and are inappropriate or off-base," he said.

Consumer advocates worry pharmaceutical companies are increasing efforts to reach teenagers through online ads.

Allergan used a "High School Musical"–type promotion for prescription acne drug Aczone featuring "Twilight" movie actor Michael Welch. He starred in an online video series called "Aczone: The Musical."

Other companies have created stuffed animals, games and children's books to promote medicines to youth, said Susan Linn, director of the Campaign for a Commercial-Free Childhood, a group of doctors, parents, teachers and other advocates.

"It's not a good idea to start kids on a life of choosing drugs based on whether they are cool, or whether some celebrity is promoting them," said Linn, who believes marketing of medicines to children should be outlawed.

Allergan spokeswoman Caroline Van Hove said the Aczone campaign was appropriate because the drug is approved for ages 12 and older. The musical website was "just one of many informational tactics" to educate patients about what at the time was the first new FDA-approved acne medicine in a decade, she said.

PhRMA's Francer said the vast majority of ads don't merit any regulatory action. He added that it can be extremely hard, especially with television commercials, to convey all of a medication's risks. "It can be incredibly challenging for the companies to present all of the risk information that both they and the FDA want to be presented in a way that is understandable to patients," he told Reuters.

"An Amazing Evening"

In Bayer's case, the New York blogger and another one in Columbus, Ohio, wrote about the parties immediately afterward, mentioning both the website that helped organize them as well as the birth control device being touted.

Although studies show that drug ads work—consumers who see them are more likely to ask their doctors about the product—it is unclear whether the company's events to promote Mirena had any impact beyond the small parties' audience.

"I went to a brunch yesterday that was hosted by Mom Central and Bayer Healthcare, and they brought in two speakers. One to talk (humorously) about their Mirena birth control product, and the other to give us 'frazzled moms' some basic style tips. . . . The speakers knew their stuff, and did a good job," read one account on www.sanemoms.com that then focused only on fashion.

Another shorter post, at www.chefdruck.blogspot.com, also only mentioned Mirena in passing in favor of tips on shoes and husbands. "We had an amazing evening, talking about sex, fashion, and living a simpler life," it said.

Stacy DeBroff, chief executive of Mom Central, likened the parties to a focus group, but said her website won't partner with any other drugmakers until the FDA clears up its rules.

"For us, it was kind of an experiment of sorts. . . . If we bring people into your living room what happens?" she told Reuters.

Still, the FDA did not find out about the Tupperware-like party pitch or the online posts until months after they hit the blogosphere and the agency received a complaint. Abrams declined to say who filed the grievance.

Bayer Healthcare, a unit of the German drugmaker Bayer AG, said it stopped holding the parties 10 months before it even received the agency's letter.

In comments to the FDA over social media policies, the German drugmaker said the agency should open up channels to market products and embrace the use of technology, not restrict it. "Any FDA approach should seek to maximize the dissemination of accurate healthcare information to patients and their caregivers," Bayer's senior counsel Christopher Cannon wrote earlier this year. The FDA, he added, should allow drugmakers to be "using the full spectrum of social media and other tools available via the Internet."

Abrams, age 55, said he personally uses Facebook but still relies on his younger staffers to keep up with technology. "I'm not that sophisticated," he joked.

He also said his division will continue to be aggressive in rooting out suspect marketing. One ad reviewer, he said, recently called in on her way to vacation in Florida, having seen a misleading television ad for an erectile dysfunction suppository at the airport.

As for Abrams, he keeps a pad of paper by his television for some evenings when he is watching with his wife, Maureen.

"I can be watching TV with my wife after our kids go to bed, and she knows . . . when a drug commercial comes on: no talking," he said.

"*Gift giving is one way in which pharmaceutical companies and their representatives attempt to influence the practice of medicine.*"

Pharmaceutical Companies Unfairly Influence Doctors with Gifts

Steven P. Higgins

In the following viewpoint, Steven P. Higgins alleges that pharmaceutical companies influence health care practitioners through gift giving. He claims that even gifts of insignificant value can shift a physician's obligations from the patient to the drug company. Higgins also expresses a concern that while accepting gifts is commonly seen as inappropriate, physicians are not likely to view themselves as susceptible to such manipulations. The author is a dermatologist and adjunct assistant professor in the Department of Dermatology at Duke University School of Medicine.

Steven P. Higgins, "Drug Representatives: Giving You Lunch or Stealing Your Soul?" *Dermatology Online Journal*, vol. 13, no. 4, 2007. Copyright © The Regents of the University of California, Davis campus and Copyright © Steven P. Higgins. Originally published in *Dermatology Online Journal*. All rights reserved. Reproduced with permission.

As you read, consider the following questions:

1. How does Higgins support his statement that even small gifts influence health care providers?

2. How do patients view drug companies' gifts to physicians, according to Higgins?

3. How do free meals influence physicians who speak at functions, in the author's opinion?

The pharmaceutical industry is one of the most profitable in the US.[1] A distinctive feature of this business is its dependence on physicians to recommend its prescription products. This necessity is underscored by the promotional budget of pharmaceutical companies, over $27 billion in 2004, mostly targeted at physicians.[1]

Gift giving is one way in which pharmaceutical companies and their representatives attempt to influence the practice of medicine. The impact of pharmaceutical representatives and gifts such as free lunches are increasingly popular topics in both the lay press and medical literature.[2,3,4,5] Fearing a conflict of interest, medical professional societies have established guidelines to help healthcare providers decide which gifts are appropriate.[6,7] Guidelines for the American Academy of Dermatology refer to those of the American Medical Association (AMA).[8] The AMA guidelines are somewhat vague, for example, stating that gifts should be "of minimal value." An attempt to clarify the guidelines set limits on gift value, such as $100, that seem arbitrary.[9]

Moreover, such limits ignore the importance of small gifts. Studies reveal that seemingly insignificant gifts can influence behavior. For example, a pharmacy that gave a keychain to all patrons noted a 17 percent increase in sales.[10] A charity fundraiser that employed direct mail solicitation had an increase in response rate from 18 percent to 35 percent when free address labels were included.[10] Gifts, even those of trivial monetary value, impart a sense of obligation that conflicts with the provider's primary responsibility to the patient. A physician who is the recipient of a gift may recommend products made by the gift-giver without due consideration of other cheaper or more effective options.

This potential conflict of interest is not lost on patients. Although physicians may balk at the suggestion that their integrity is compromised by the acceptance of trinkets such as pens and notepads, a third of patients surveyed believe that the receipt of any gift compels a physician to prescribe a particular product.[11] For all types of gifts except drug samples, patients are consistently more likely than physicians to think the gift is influential.[11] This could compromise trust in the physician-patient relationship, whether or not the gift ultimately influences the physician. Furthermore, time constraints of typical patient encounters dictate that most physicians are unlikely to disclose all drug company-related gifts to their patients.

Providers perceive that drug companies successfully manipulate practices of other practitioners, yet deny that the companies' promotional efforts impact themselves (Fig.1). Although 33 percent of medicine residents acknowledge a significant effect on the habits of their peers, just 1 percent feel the efforts of pharmaceutical representatives greatly impact their own prescribing habits.[12] Similarly, 61 percent think the drug reps exert no influence on their own practice, while only 16 percent assume that other physicians are not influenced.[12] In addition, the likelihood that residents believe they are influenced by promotional items decreases with the number of items accepted.[13] Even when residents recognize gifts as inappropriate, they often take them anyway.[12] More than half of residents admit they would be unlikely to maintain the same degree of contact with pharmaceutical representatives if not for free lunches and other promotional items.[13]

Not Beholden to Pharma

Physicians work hard, but we are also well paid. We do not need to rely on 'gifts' and favours. We can buy our own pens and Post-It pads, and refuse to sell ourselves as walking billboards. We can choose not to meet pharmaceutical representatives, or read marketing materials and advertisements. We need not be beholden to Pharma for our education.

Richelle Cooper and Jerome Hoffman,
"Selling Drugs to Doctors,"
British Journal of General Practice, *February 2002*

Residents are not the only physicians potentially swayed by pharmaceutical funding. Physicians in leadership positions, who influence the decisions of other physicians, may themselves be influenced by the pharmaceutical industry. Physicians recommending formulary additions are more likely to have received drug company money to attend or speak at symposia or perform research (odds ratio 5.1, 2.0–13.2).[14] Over half of authors of clinical practice guidelines have preexisting relationships with companies producing drugs reviewed in the guidelines.[15]

Pharmaceutical representatives often provide meals at which well-known physicians are paid to speak, in the name of education. The objectivity of these speakers is arguably compromised by their honoraria and a sense of loyalty to the industry representatives at the rear of the room. A physician who portrays the featured drug unfavorably will not have a future opportunity to "educate" other providers on behalf of the company. When representatives themselves give the lectures, all inaccurate statements are favorable to the drugs being promoted.[16]

Lunches, pens, and other promotional items all play a role in drug marketing, but pharmaceutical companies spend over half of their promotional budget, 15.9 billion dollars in 2004, on samples.[1] Drug samples, seemingly a gift that would benefit patients, likely serve to make health care more expensive. Patients who finish their samples may fill costly prescriptions for the same products, unaware of inexpensive, generic alternatives. Resident physicians with access to samples are more likely to prescribe advertised medications and less likely to recommend generally cheaper over-the-counter options.[17] Medical institutions including Yale, Stanford, and the University of Pennsylvania have taken steps to limit relations between member healthcare providers and pharmaceutical companies.[18,19] However, not all institutions have sought to create distance between themselves and pharmaceutical representatives. The Weill Cornell Medical College recently opened the Clinique Skin Wellness Center, mostly financed by a $4.75 million grant from Clinique, at which patients may make on-site appointments with Clinique representatives.[20] The ends may justify the means, as one of the stated goals of the clinic is educating patients on skin cancer prevention.[20] However, physicians at that institution may have a difficult time convincing patients and others that the care they deliver is unbiased.

Mounting evidence suggests that physicians are vulnerable to various pharmaceutical marketing strategies. The fact that industry annually spends billions of dollars on advertising geared to physicians implies that such advertising is effective. The most direct way for physicians to avoid a conflict of interest with pharmaceutical companies is to eschew all types of gifts from those companies. Some feel that interactions with pharmaceutical representatives are too useful to abandon. Those providers who continue to interact with drug reps should view all gifts with skepticism, avoid the appearance of impropriety, and exercise caution to prevent compromise of the patient-physician relationship.

Acknowledgment: I would like to thank the No Free Lunch organization, www.nofreelunch.org, for providing many useful resources, including several of the references cited in this paper.

Notes

1. Kaiser Family Foundation. Trends and Indicators in the Changing Health Care Marketplace. Publication number 7031, updated February 8, 2006.
2. Saul S. Gimme an rx! Cheerleaders pep up drug sales. New York Times.2005 Nov 28.
3. Saul S. Drug makers pay for lunch as the pitch. NY Times(Print). 2006 Jul 28;A1, C7. PMID:16909492.
4. Wazana A. Physicians and the pharmaceutical industry: is a gift ever just a gift? JAMA. 2000 Jan 19;283(3):373–80. PMID: 10647801.
5. Brennan TA, Rothman DJ, Blank L, Blumenthal D, Chimonas SC, Cohen JJ, Goldman J, Kassirer JP, Kimball H, Naughton J, Smelser N. Health industry practices that create conflicts of interest: a policy proposal for academic medical centers. JAMA 2006 Jan 25;295(4):429–33. PMID: 16434633.
6. Coyle SL, Ethics and Human Rights Committtee, American College of Physicians–American Society of Internal Medicine. Physician-industry relations. Part 1: individual physicians. Ann Intern Med. 2002 Mar 5;136(5):396–402. PMID: 11874314.
7. American Medical Association Ethical Opinions and Guidelines Opinion 8.061, "Gifts to Physicians from Industry," updated 26 Jan 2005, www.ama-assn.org/ama/pub/category/4001.html.
8. AAD Code of Medical Ethics for Dermatologists, Approved 12/3/05, Revised 11/4/06, www.aad.org.professionals/policies/ar.htm.
9. American Medical Association Opinion E-8.061: clarifying addendum, updated June 2002, www.ama-assn.org/ama/pub/category/4263.html.

10. Katz D, Caplan AL, Merz JF. All gifts large and small: toward an understanding of the ethics of pharmaceutical industry gift-giving. Am J Bioeth. 2003 Summer;3(3):39–46. PMID: 14594489.

11. Gibbons, RV, Landry FJ, Blouch DL, Jones DL, Williams FK, Lucey CR, Kroenke K. A comparison of physicians' and patients' attitudes toward pharmaceutical industry gifts. J Gen Intern Med. 1998 Mar;13(3):151–4. PMID: 9541370.

12. Steinman MA, Shlipak MC, McPhee SJ. Of principles and pens: attitudes and practices of medicine housestaff toward pharmaceutical industry promotions. Am J Med. 2001 May;110(7):551:–7. PMID: 11347622.

13. Hodges B. Interactions with the pharmaceutical industry: experiences and attitudes of psychiatry residents, interns and clerks. CMAJ. 1995 Sep 1;153(5):553–9. PMID: 7641153.

14. Chren MM, Landefeld CS. Physicians' behavior and their interactions with drug companies: a controlled study of physicians who requested additions to a hospital formulary. JAMA. 1994 Mar 2:271(9):684–9. PMID: 8309031.

15. Choudhry NK, Stelfox HT, Detsky AS. Relationships between authors of clinical practice guidelines and the pharmaceutical industry. JAMA. 2002 Feb 6;287(5):612–7. PMID: 11829700.

16. Ziegler MG, Lew P, Singer BC. The accuracy of drug information from pharmaceutical sales representatives. JAMA. 1995 Apr 26;273(16):1296–8. PMID: 7715044.

17. Adair RF, Holmgren LR. Do drug samples influence resident prescribing behavior? A randomized trial. Am J Med. 2005 Aug;118(8):881–4. PMID: 16084181.

18. Pollack A. Stanford to ban drug makers' gifts to doctors, even pens. NY Times (Print). 2006 Sep 12:C2. PMID: 16972375.

19. Coleman DL, Kazdin AE, Miller LA, Morrow JS, Udelsman R. Guidelines for interactions between clincial faculty and the pharmaceutical industry: one medical school's approach. Acad Med. 2006 Feb;81(2):154–60. PMID: 16436576.
20. Singer N. Skin deep, a word from our sponsor. New York Times. 2007 Jan 25.

"*Most relationships [between doctors and pharmaceutical companies] are legitimate.*"

Most Pharmaceutical Companies Have Legitimate Relationships with Doctors

Bradley P. Knight

In the following viewpoint, Bradley P. Knight defends the relationships between the pharmaceutical industry and health care providers. Knight agrees that gifts from drug companies to physicians create conflicts of interests that must be controlled, but he points out that media coverage unfairly demonizes such relationships. In contrast, the author distinguishes two types of relationships physicians have with drug and medical device companies: those with the potential for financial, professional, or personal gain and those with legitimate consultation practices and participation in clinical trials. Knight is director of electrophysiology at Northwestern University's Feinberg School of Medicine and editor in chief of EP Lab Digest.

Bradley P. Knight, "In Defense of Legitimate Relationships Between Physicians and Industry," *EP Lab Digest E-Newsletter*, vol. 10, no. 12, December 1, 2010. Copyright © HMP Communications. All rights reserved. Reproduced with permission.

As you read, consider the following questions:

1. What is Knight's response to the argument that physicians should not receive gifts from the industry?

2. What examples does the author provide of legitimate interactions between physicians and drug companies?

3. What is the impact of restricting medical field leaders from participating in legitimate activities with the industry, in Knight's view?

There has been a great deal of negative attention lately to relationships between physicians and [the drug and medical device] industry. A front-page story in the *Chicago Tribune* newspaper in October [2010] was devoted to a list of all physicians in the Chicago area who received over $100,000 in compensation from the pharmaceutical industry in the past year. It does seem that something is awry when an individual practicing physician earns $250,000 from a drug company, but the reactions by the media, legislators, and some professional medical associations (PMAs) have demonized all relationships between physicians and industry.

Controlling Conflicts of Interest

Last year [2009], the *Journal of the American Medical Association* (JAMA) published a proposal for controlling conflicts of interest between PMAs and their relationships with industry. It described several underlying principles and premises, and provided some valid suggestions. Most of these are intuitive. For example, most physicians would agree with the following:

1. "The pharmaceutical and medical device industries make important contributions to medical progress." No one in the highly technology-dependent field of electrophysiology can argue against this. The pacemakers and defibrillators we implant, the tools that we use during

catheter ablation procedures, and the antiarrhythmic drugs that we prescribe have all been developed by industry. Often these devices were found to be effective through industry-sponsored clinical trials involving practicing electrophysiologists.

2. Physicians should fully disclose financial relationships with industry. Full disclosure and transparency is now widely endorsed. However, "resolving issues of conflict of interest is not best accomplished by avoiding all relationships."

3. Physicians should not receive gifts from industry. "Research demonstrates the power of gifts to bias physicians' choices." There have been rules against physicians accepting gifts for several years now.

4. "Funds from industry (to PMAs) should be unrestricted." Physicians are able to easily identify when industry support comes with strings attached.

5. "Physicians and medical societies should avoid marketing industry products." Academic institutions and physicians who are involved in industry-sponsored educational activities have defined which activities are related to product marketing and should be avoided, and which activities are supported by unrestricted industry funding and are acceptable.

However, the JAMA article makes recommendations to restrict who can serve on PMA Professional Guideline and Scientific Session committees that are unnecessary and fail to recognize that most relationships are legitimate. They state that "disclosure of industry relationships by committee members is not sufficient protection.... At a minimum, PMAs must exclude from such committees persons with any conflict of interest ($0 threshold) involving direct salary support, re-

Physicians Don't Feel DTC Ads Impact Prescribing Habits

[T]he majority of physicians do not feel that DTC advertising has pressured them to prescribe inappropriate medications—or, indeed, that it has pressured them to prescribe at all. Most consumers who consult their doctor about an advertised drug are not even seeking a specific prescription. They want information about an underlying condition and available treatment.

Pat Kelly, "Perspective: DTC Advertising's Benefits Far Outreigh Its Imperfections," Health Affairs, 2004.

search support, or additional income from a company whose product sales could be affected by the guidelines."

Not All Relationships Created Equal

These zero tolerance recommendations regarding committee membership fail to differentiate two very separate types of relationships between physicians and companies: those that are real conflicts of interest and those that could be perceived [as such]. Not all relationships with industry are created equal. A real conflict of interest should be defined as one where the person or a member of the person's household, has a reasonable potential for financial, professional, or other personal gain or loss as a result of the issues or content addressed by the committee. Obvious examples are when physicians are company employees, receive direct salary support, own company stock or stock options, or receive royalties. In these cases the physician has potential for future additional income based on the success of the company. In contrast, physicians who provide legitimate advice to a company, participate in industry-sponsored clinical trials, or are involved in an unrestricted industry-sponsored educational activity are not in a position to directly gain personally in the future based on the financial success of the company. The latter activities should be encouraged, fostered, and promoted, and physicians involved in these activities should not be restricted from being involved in leadership positions and roles in medical societies. It only makes sense that physicians should continue to work directly with companies to develop better products used for patent care. And it only makes sense that these physicians should be compensated for their efforts. These activities are not the same as making an investment in a company.

Restricting leaders in our field from participating in legitimate activities with industry only perpetuates the misperceptions in the media and by the public that all relationships between physicians and industry are illegitimate or suspect, and that physicians can be persuaded to deviate from the best possible medical care. It is clear that receiving gifts has been shown to influence physician prescribing patterns, but where is the evidence that consulting for a company alters clinical decision making? Perceptions are important, but inaccurate perceptions should be addressed by education and awareness. Physicians should discourage real conflicts of interest, but should also be proud of the accomplishments that have been made for patients as a result of productive and honest relationships with industry.

It is important for the public to know that if they ever have to undergo a heart rhythm procedure, there will likely be a company representative in the procedure room. This person will be there to provide inventory, optimize device programming, facilitate cardiac mapping, and provide expertise. It is also important that the public understands that it is critical that physicians continue to work with the companies that make these devices to improve the care of patients with heart rhythm disorders.

Periodical and Internet Sources Bibliography

The following articles have been selected to supplement the diverse views presented in this chapter.

Peter Conrad and Valerie Leiter	"From Lydia Pinkham to Queen Levitra: Direct-to-Consumer Advertising and Medicalisation," *Sociology of Health & Illness*, September 2008.
Carl Elliot	"The Secret Lives of Big Pharma's 'Thought Leaders,'" *Chronicle Review*, September 12, 2010.
Jeremy A. Greene and Aaron S. Kesselheim	"Pharmaceutical Marketing and the New Social Media," *New England Journal of Medicine*, November 24, 2010.
Sean Gregory	"Are Direct-to-Consumer Drug Ads Doomed?," *Time*, February 4, 2009.
Mindy Jung	"Physicians Are Talking About: The Not-So-Simple Gifts from Pharmaceutical Companies," Medscape, July 8, 2010. www.medscape.com.
Brian A. Liang and Timothy Mackey	"Direct-to-Consumer Advertising with Interactive Internet Media," *Journal of the American Medical Association*, February 23, 2011.
Mukesh Mehta	"Pharmaceutical Marketing After the Gold Rush," *Next Generation Pharmaceutical*, March 2010.
Scott Moldenhauer	"In Defense of the Battered Sales Rep," PharmExec.com, July 1, 2010. www.pharmexec.findpharma.com.
Megan Tady	"Tracking Pharma Gifts to Doctors," *American Prospect*, August 9, 2007.

Is the Cost of Prescription Drugs in America Appropriate?

Chapter Preface

Generics can cost up to 90 percent less than brand-name or "innovator" drugs and account for more than 70 percent of prescriptions taken in the United States. To be approved by the Food and Drug Administration (FDA), a generic must be identical to the innovator in its active ingredient, potency, dosage form, and route of administration. It also must have the same use indications, be equal in therapeutic effect and time frame (bioequivalent), and meet a matching set of batch requirements (identity, strength, quality, and purity). Finally, a generic must be manufactured under the FDA standards and regulations applied to the brand-name drug.

Nonetheless, a small number of patients who have switched to generics have experienced negative reactions or side effects. For instance, when Sassee Ann Arnold began taking a copycat version of Synthroid for her underactive thyroid, her condition immediately worsened. "I hated climbing the stairs to go to bed at night," Arnold says. "The pain would shoot down to my left leg to my feet. I would get charley horses in my toes and feet. My hair started falling out."[1] Her health quickly returned to normal after switching back to Synthroid.

Such instances can occur with a prescription that has a "narrow therapeutic window," meaning that even the slightest change in dosage can spell the difference between inefficacy and toxicity. In fact, the inactive "filler" ingredients in generics are allowed to differ from the innovator. "The FDA quite rigidly states that when they say a drug is substitutable, they mean that with no caveats, no qualifications," maintains Peter

1. Quoted in Elisabeth Leamy, "Generic Drugs Are Much Cheaper, but Use Caution for Those That Have 'Narrow Therapeutic Windows,'" ABC News, October http://abcnews.go.com/GMA/ConsumerNews/generic-drugs-cheaper-caution/story?id=8925388.

Meredith, a pharmacologist at the University of Glasgow in Scotland. "My concern would be that if you don't look for one, you don't see it."[2] Nonetheless, the administration insists that the vast majority of generics are just as safe and effective as brand-name drugs. "FDA receives very few reports of adverse events about specific generic drugs," it claims. "In most cases, reports of adverse events generally describe a known reaction to the active drug ingredient."[3] The authors in the following chapter debate whether pharmaceuticals are worth their current prices.

2. Quoted in Melissa Healy, "Are Generics Just as Good?," *Los Angeles Times*, March 17, 2008. http://articles.latimes.com/2008/mar/17/health/he-generic17/3.
3. Food and Drug Administration, "Myths and Facts About Generic Drugs," October 13, 2009. www.fda.gov/Drugs/ResourcesForYou/Consumers/BuyingUsingMedicineSafely/UnderstandingGenericDrugs/ucm167991.htm.

> *"Economic studies have shown that even the newer, more expensive drugs are usually worth their price."*

The Cost of Prescription Drugs Is Appropriate

Charles L. Hooper

Charles L. Hooper is president of Objective Insights, a company specializing in pharmaceutical and biotech consultation, and a visiting fellow with the Hoover Institution. In the following viewpoint, he maintains that prescription costs are appropriate relative to the larger picture of development and economics. Bringing new medicines to the market, Hooper states, is highly expensive because of the strict, slow review process of the Food and Drug Administration. He adds that bulk purchasers— foreign countries, the federal government, hospitals—seeking the lowest prices impact how pharmaceutical companies price their drugs. Overall, newer and costlier drugs are more effective than generics, over-the-counter medications, and other treatments and actually reduce health care costs, Hooper concludes.

Charles L. Hooper, "Pharmaceuticals: Economics and Regulation," *The Concise Encyclopedia of Economics*, 2008. Copyright © Liberty Fund, Inc. All rights reserved. Reproduced with permission.

As you read, consider the following questions:

1. How do individual governments affect drug prices, in the author's opinion?

2. What prevents pharmaceutical companies from aiding the poor, as stated by Hooper?

3. In the author's view, how does insurance impact spending on prescription and generic drugs?

A study by Joseph DiMasi, an economist at the Tufts Center for the Study of Drug Development in Boston, found that the cost of getting one new drug approved was $802 million in 2000 U.S. dollars. Most new drugs cost much less, but his figure adds in each successful drug's prorated share of failures. Only one out of fifty drugs eventually reaches the market.

Why are drugs so expensive to develop? The main reason for the high cost is the . . . high level of proof required by the Food and Drug Administration [FDA]. Before it will approve a new drug, the FDA requires pharmaceutical companies to carefully test it in animals and then humans in the standard phases 0, I, II, and III process. The path through the FDA's review process is slow and expensive. The ten to fifteen years required to get a drug through the testing and approval process leaves little remaining time on a twenty-year patent.

Although new medicines are hugely expensive to bring to market, they are cheap to manufacture. In this sense, they are like DVD movies and computer software. This means that a drug company, to be profitable or simply to break even, must price its drugs well above its production costs. The company that wishes to maximize profits will set high prices for those who are willing to pay a lot and low prices that at least cover production costs for those willing to pay a little. That is why, for example, Merck priced its anti-AIDS drug, Crixivan, to poor countries in Africa and Latin America at $600 while charging relatively affluent Americans $6,099 for a year's supply.

This type of customer segmentation—similar to that of airlines—is part of the profit-maximizing strategy for medicines. In general, good customer segmentation is difficult to accomplish. Therefore, the most common type of pharmaceutical segmentation is charging a lower price in poorer countries and giving the product free to poor people in the United States through patient assistance programs.

What complicates the picture is socialized medicine, which exists in almost every country outside the United States—and even, with Medicare and Medicaid, in the United States. Because governments in countries with socialized medicine tend to be the sole bargaining agent in dealing with drug companies, these governments often set prices that are low by U.S. standards. To some extent, this comes about because these governments have monopsony power [single influence on pricing]—that is, monopoly power on the buyer's side—and they use this power to get good deals. These governments are, in effect, saying that if they cannot buy it cheaply, their citizens cannot get it.

These low prices also come about because governments sometimes threaten drug companies with compulsory licensing (breaking a patent) to get a low price. This has happened most recently in South Africa and Brazil with AIDS drugs. This violation of intellectual property rights can bring a seemingly powerful drug company into quick compliance. When faced with a choice between earning nothing and earning something, most drug companies choose the latter.

A Prisoner's Dilemma

The situation is a prisoner's dilemma. Everyone's interest is in giving drug companies an adequate incentive to invest in new drugs. To do so, drug companies must be able to price their drugs well above production costs to a large segment of the population. But each individual government's narrow self-interest is to set a low price on drugs and let people in other countries pay the high prices that generate the return on R&D [research and development] investments. Each government, in other words, has an incentive to be a free rider. And that is what many governments are doing. The temptation is to cease having Americans bear more than their share of drug development by having the U.S. government set low prices also. But if Americans also try to free ride, there may not be a ride.

Governments are not the only bulk purchasers. The majority of pharmaceuticals in the United States are purchased by managed-care organizations (MCOs), hospitals, and governments, which use their market power to negotiate better prices. These organizations often do not take physical possession of the drugs; most pills never pass through the MCO's hands, but instead go from manufacturer to wholesaler to pharmacy to patient. Therefore, manufacturers rebate money—billions of dollars—to compensate for purchases made at list prices. Managed-care rebates are given with consideration; they are the result of contracts that require performance. For example, a manufacturer will pay an HMO [health maintenance organization] a rebate if it can keep a drug's prescription market share above the national level. These rebates average 10–40 percent of sales. The net result is that the neediest Americans, frequently those without insurance, pay the highest prices, while the most powerful health plans and government agencies pay the lowest.

Pharmaceutical companies would like to help poor people in the United States, but the federal government and, to a much lesser extent, health plans have tied their hands. Drug companies can and do give drugs away free through patient assistance programs, but they cannot sell them at very low prices because the federal government requires drug companies to give the huge Medicaid program their "best prices." If a drug company sells to even one customer at a very low price, it also has to sell at the same price to the 5–40 percent of its customers covered by Medicaid.

Worth Their Price

Drug prices are regularly attacked as "too high." Yet, cheaper over-the-counter drugs, natural medicines, and generic versions of off-patent drugs are ubiquitous, and many health plans steer patients toward them. Economic studies have shown that even the newer, more expensive drugs are usually worth their price and are frequently cheaper than other alternatives. One study showed that each dollar spent on vaccines reduced other health care costs by $10. Another study showed that for each dollar spent on newer drugs, $6.17 was saved. Therefore, health plans that aggressively limited their drug spending ended up spending *more* over all.

Most patients do not pay retail prices because they have some form of insurance. In 2003, before a law was passed that subsidizes drugs for seniors, 75–80 percent of seniors had prescription drug insurance. Insured people pay either a flat co-payment, often based on tiers (copayment levels set by managed-care providers that involve a low payment for generic drugs and a higher payment for brand-name drugs) or a percentage of the prescription cost. On average, seniors spend more on entertainment than they do on drugs and medical supplies combined. But for the uninsured who are also poor and sick, drug prices can be a devastating burden. The overlap of the 20–25 percent who lack drug insurance and the 10 percent who pay more than five thousand dollars per year— approximately 2 percent are in both groups—is where we find the stories of people skimping on food to afford their medications. The number of people in both groups is actually lower than 2 percent because of the numerous patient assistance programs offered by pharmaceutical companies. For all the talk of lower drug prices, what people really want is lower risk through good insurance.

Insurance lowers an individual's risk and, consequently, increases the demand for pharmaceuticals. By spending someone else's money for a good chunk of every pharmaceutical purchase, individuals become less price sensitive. A two-hundred-dollar prescription for a new medicine is forty times as expensive as a five-dollar generic, but its copay may be only three times the generic's copay. The marginal cost to patients of choosing the expensive product is reduced, both in absolute and relative terms, and patients are thus more likely to purchase the expensive drug and make purchases they otherwise would have skipped. The data show that those with insurance consume 40–100 percent more than those without insurance.

Drugs account for a small percentage of overall health-care spending. In fact, branded pharmaceuticals are about 7 percent and generics 3 percent of total U.S. health-care costs. The tremendous costs involved with illnesses—even if they are not directly measured—are the economic and human costs of the diseases themselves, not the drugs.

> *"Prices of prescription drugs continue to soar in the United States . . . [so] many Americans rely on online pharmacies for their prescription medication."*

The High Cost of Prescription Drugs Forces People to Buy Online from Risky Foreign Pharmacies

PRWeb Newswire

In the following viewpoint, PRWeb Newswire states that prescription drug prices are higher in the United States than in other countries. The increasing cost of prescription drugs has led to many Americans' purchasing their medications from Canadian online pharmacies where the drugs are cheaper. As a result, Americans need to be aware of which sites selling prescription medications may be fraudulent. PRWeb Newswire is a leader in online publicity and online news distribution.

As you read, consider the following questions:

1. What is a difficulty Americans may face when purchasing prescription medications online, according to the author?

2. What is one clue as stated by PRWeb Newswire that would be a sign that a site may be fraudulent.

3. What is the CIPA, as described by the author?

While prices of prescription drugs continue to soar in the United States, they still remain at the usual low costs just across the border in Canada and other parts of the world. Many Americans rely on online pharmacies for their prescription medication. Unfortunately, with the overwhelming number of fraudulent businesses that taint the internet market, it can be difficult to determine which sites you can trust. When purchasing medication from online pharmacies it is critical that you order from legitimate and reputable sites, avoiding those businesses engaged in fraudulent operations.

Clues to Fraudulent Pharmacies

Separating the good pharmacy sites from the bad ones may not be as challenging a task as it may seem. There are some sure-tell signs that distinguish these fake businesses from the registered international pharmacies they claim to be. One of the biggest giveaways of fraudulent pharmacies is that they do not require a prescription for purchasing a prescription medication. According to the federal Food and Drug Administration, it is a violation of the law to dispense prescription medications without a legitimate prescription. The practice of distributing medications without a prescription can put a patient at a serious health risk.

Another sign that a site may be a fraud is lack of contact information. Over 90 percent of online pharmacies do not offer a phone number or address as contact information. This lack of information can say a lot about a pharmacy. If the pharmacy prefers to remain anonymous it may be a sign they have something to hide. If this is the case, it is in your best interest to purchase your medication at a different online pharmacy as this is a probable sign of fraud. A legitimate pharmacy will provide its customers with full contact information.

Furthermore, Pharmacy Checker is an association which verifies the credentials of online pharmacies. Pharmacy Checker is dedicated to evaluating sites and providing customer feedback to ensure that consumers are receiving medications from safe and qualified establishments. When looking for sites to buy medications from, check for the Pharmacy Checker stamp of approval logo.

The CIPA Seal

The Canadian International Pharmacy Association, also known as CIPA, is another regulatory body that registers legitimate Canadian online pharmacies. CIPA has strict standards to ensure the quality, safety and handling of the prescriptions dispensed by each of the pharmacies it certifies. These pharmacies are licensed and regulated by the government for safety. All valid Canadian online pharmacies that are registered through CIPA will display the CIPA seal on their home page.

Americans shopping online for prescription medications should be aware of and engaged in looking for these indicators of either legitimate or fraudulent pharmacies. Once a pharmacy's authenticity has been verified, a customer should feel confident about the quality of their medication. Quality prescriptiondrugs.com is one of Canada's highest rated, fully licensed online pharmacies and provides thousands of customers with safe and affordable medication. Quality Prescription Drugs requires a prescription from all patients who are purchasing prescription medication and does not provide narcotics or controlled substances. Licensed by CIPA and approved by Pharmacy Checker, they supply patients with genuine and safe medications.

Qualityprescriptiondrugs.com is an online pharmacy that is certified by Pharmacy Checker and CIPA. In the 7 years of the company's operation, Qualityprescriptiondrugs.com has never had a case of fraudulent medication. Qualityprescrip tiondrugs.com offers Americans savings of up to 70% on their prescriptions.

"In 2007, the tab for bioengineered and 'specialty' drugs was nearly $59 billion. Industry analysts predict it will reach $98 billion by 2011."

The Cost of Specialty Prescription Drugs Is Too High

Carol M. Ostrom

Carol M. Ostrom is a staff reporter for the Seattle Times. *In the following viewpoint, she writes that emerging specialty drugs pose a financial burden to patients and employers who pay for their insurance coverage alike. Unlike the average pill, specialty drugs are bioengineered, painstaking to replicate, and targeted to chronic conditions, compounding their costs, Ostrom states. Furthermore, Medicare and a growing number of insurance plans, she contends, now require patients to pay a large percentage of the cost of these medications, which can total thousands of dollars monthly. For employers, Ostrom continues, specialty drugs may raise insurance premiums and threaten the affordability of offering employee health benefits.*

As you read, consider the following questions:

1. According to Ostrom, how does the pharmaceutical industry respond to accusations of price gouging?

2. What ethical dilemma do specialty drugs pose to employers, in the author's view?

3. How did specialty drugs affect insurers' cost-sharing tiers for drugs, as stated by Ostrom?

Sally Garcia, a 53-year-old lawyer disabled by multiple sclerosis, was torn.

A new-generation medication, Copaxone, was really working for her. After two decades of being in and out of hospitals, Garcia was taking steps to work again.

Her wallet, though, was in severe distress. Under her Medicare prescription plan, Garcia's share of the expensive drug was $330 per month. All together, medications were taking a third of her disability payments—her only income—and she couldn't swing it.

Copaxone, Enbrel, Remicade: For some patients, such new-generation drugs, often called "biologicals" or "bioengineered" when they are created by genetically modified living cells, have performed magic. In some cases, they work when other drugs have failed, or for diseases that previously had no drug treatments at all.

But they cost a lot—often $2,000 to $3,000 per month.

And in a double whammy, some insured patients who previously paid a fixed amount—likely $30 to $50 even for the most expensive, brand-name drugs—are suddenly finding the rules have changed.

For these new drugs, an increasing number of patients must pay a percentage of the tab, generally 25 to 30 percent. For many of those patients, that can mean a bill of $600 to $900 a month for a drug that they may need for many years.

The rising bill for such complex drugs threatens to financially overwhelm patients and employers, and—if current trends continue—to unravel the very philosophy of health insurance.

"The idea of insurance is to protect people from catastrophic costs," says Gary Claxton, director of the Healthcare Marketplace Project for the Kaiser Family Foundation.

"At some point, people aren't going to consider themselves insured if they're at risk for a huge amount out-of-pocket just because they have one disease rather than another."

Usage Expected to Soar

Today, such drugs are prescribed relatively rarely. But their use is expected to explode.

In 2007, the tab for bioengineered and "specialty" drugs was nearly $59 billion. Industry analysts predict it will reach $98 billion by 2011.

"The reality is that this is where the pharmaceutical industry is focusing their research," says Jim Carlson, Group Health Cooperative's pharmacy director.

The pharmaceutical industry long has been accused of price gouging and producing "new" drugs that aren't better than cheaper ones already on the market, and it has been criticized for its direct-to-patient advertising.

In response, the industry points to long periods of expensive research and development that often end without new products. Healthy profits attract investors to fund new research, it argues, and advertising helps patients make informed choices.

The emergence of bioengineered drugs has dramatically magnified these disputes. Most are produced through complicated, delicate procedures that are difficult to replicate.

Unlike a typical oral pill, the new bioengineered drugs have no simple chemical "recipe" that can be easily followed by another company. In fact, the federal Food and Drug Administration has no process yet for creating a generic version, in this world often called a "bio-similar."

Most often given as injections for diseases such as advanced breast cancer, rheumatoid arthritis or MS, bioengineered drugs can be lifesavers.

"The costs might be out of the ballpark, but in the past, without that drug, the person might not be living or not living any type of quality of life," says SuAnn Stone, director of pharmacy services for Regence BlueShield, one of Washington's largest insurers.

For patients and employers, the costs can be huge, particularly since many are targeted at chronic diseases that can require long-term treatment.

Typical bioengineered drug treatments for rheumatoid arthritis now run about $16,000 a year, says Dr. Philip Mease, director of rheumatology research for Swedish Medical Center.

At Premera Blue Cross, another large local insurer, such unique "specialty" drugs account for 1 percent of pharmacy claims, but 15 percent of the costs.

Because such specialty drugs are so expensive, most Medicare "Part D" prescription-drug plans and a small but increasing number of private insurance plans have isolated them—either by type or by price—into a separate category that requires patients to pay more. Usually, the patient is asked to pick up a percentage of the cost, rather than a fixed co-payment.

Patients with chronic illnesses, who could need the drug for years, are getting hit hardest by the change, says Dan Mendelson, president of Avalere Health, a national health-policy analysis firm.

"It gets to the fundamental question of 'What is insurance?'" he said.

As advances in medicine become ever more costly, insurance that requires heavy cost-sharing from patients for pricey drugs is likely a "microcosm of medicine's future," predicts a commentary in a recent *New England Journal of Medicine.*

The authors warn: "At some point in our lives, we may all join that small pool of users of high-cost care."

Ethical Dilemma

Traci Ohlsen, a nurse, had rheumatoid arthritis as a child, but the crippling disease was in remission for years. Seven years ago, it came back hard, attacking her back, hips, neck and hands, and producing debilitating fatigue.

She tried several biotech drugs but couldn't tolerate the side effects. Finally, she tried Orencia, given by intravenous infusion in a doctor's office.

Her doctor prescribed three infusions, at $4,500 each. After two, she began feeling well enough to return to part-time work.

But Ohlsen, 44, of Renton, recently put off the third infusion when her insurer balked. She realized she might already owe $9,000, she said, and didn't want to add to the tab.

"If I end up having to pay for those last two infusions . . . I would have to file for bankruptcy," she said.

As costly drugs become more commonly prescribed, employers, who buy most private health insurance, are watching warily.

"They want to keep employees and be good employers, but there is a lot of pressure on the cost of health care right now," said Group Health Cooperative spokesman Michael Foley.

Everyone recognizes the ethical dilemma: Do you make the sickest pay the most, or do you require everyone to foot the bill? Will costs raise premiums so much that some employers drop drug coverage or even health insurance itself?

Some insurers argue that requiring patients to pay a percentage keeps the patient's share more proportionate to the drug costs, and therefore more fair—and more tolerable to employers.

"We're trying to make sure that the benefit is kept affordable for the other 1,000 employees in the company," said Susan Pisano, spokeswoman for America's Health Insurance Plans, an industry group.

That group says doctors sometimes prefer newer drugs even with scant evidence that they work better than older, less-expensive drugs.

"Is a drug that costs 100 times more . . . 100 times better?" Pisano asked. "Today, we don't know, because there is no independent entity that makes those comparisons."

Insurers in Washington

In the recent past, most insurance plans covered prescription drugs in three "tiers," requiring flat co-payments ranging from $5 or $10 for generics to several times that for brand-name drugs not "preferred" by the insurer.

But that appears to be changing, with Medicare Part D plans, the stand-alone prescription drug plans set up by Congress in 2003, leading the way.

Now, 86 percent of such plans have a "fourth tier" requiring higher cost-sharing—up to 33 percent—for more expensive drugs, according to the Kaiser Family Foundation.

About 10 percent of commercial plans now have a specialty-drug tier, Mendelson says.

In Washington, two smaller insurers, Aetna and United Health Group, have created a fourth tier in some plans.

Even without fourth tiers, some plans require high cost-sharing for brand-name drugs, particularly if they aren't "preferred." For example, Regence BlueShield and Premera Blue Cross offer plans requiring patients to pay 50 percent of top-tier drugs' costs.

About 78,000 of Premera's 1.4 million members statewide have group or individual plans that require them to pay a percentage for some drugs. A minority of those plans limit yearly out-of-pocket expenses to $10,000.

Sometimes injectable biotech drugs are covered under medical benefits because they require doctor visits. That's typically true for the asthma drug Xolair, which can cost $30,000 a year, and some arthritis biotech drugs.

Insurers say that when there's convincing evidence a drug works better, it's moved to their "preferred" list.

But insurers can disagree. For example, Tykerb, for advanced breast cancer, is a preferred drug at Premera but not at Regence.

And for patients, the rules can get really confusing.

Jeanne Sather, 53, a 10-year cancer survivor in Seattle who lives on Social Security disability payments, recently discovered that her new Medicare Part D plan required her to pay $1,600 a month for Tykerb.

That would leave her $900 a month to live on.

"For me, Tykerb is a fabulous drug," Sather said. " . . . But obviously, I can't pay this."

Escalating cost-sharing tiers for drugs originally were developed to encourage patients to use lower-cost generics or "therapeutically equivalent" brands, noted Claxton, of the Healthcare Marketplace Project.

But, with the development of costly bioengineered drugs, insurers may have found a new use for the tier system.

When patients have no less-expensive choice, Avalere's Mendelson argues, cost tiers simply punish patients instead of encouraging thrifty, healthy behavior.

"These tiering policies don't accomplish that. They just stick it to the chronically ill."

The Future: Tough Choices

As bioengineered drugs become more widely used, industry observers predict more employers will adopt percentage cost-sharing.

At SeaBright Insurance in Seattle, Gene Gerrard, the assistant vice president of human resources, says prescription drugs make up 24 percent of the company's health-care spending.

In the future, he says, his employees will have to have "a little more skin in the game," but so far, it's not clear how much. Still, he adds: "We have to recognize that we can only spend so much on health care."

That means tough choices.

For example, the state spends $25 million a year on life-saving specialty drugs for 30 patients with hemophilia, says Dr. Jeffery Thompson, chief medical officer for the state's Medicaid program. "What are the options? Other than turn off the lights and say goodbye?"

In large part, the looming cost issue of specialty drugs has been masked by the increasing use of cheaper generic drugs.

But with unique drugs, insurers have little bargaining power, they say.

Patients should have access to the best available therapies, said Pisano, the insurance-industry spokeswoman.

But, she added: "In some instances, manufacturers are charging exorbitant prices for single-source drugs, and prices keep increasing dramatically."

Dr. Peter McGough, former president of the Washington State Medical Association, and now chief medical officer for UW Medicine's neighborhood clinics, recalls the time decades ago in Seattle when kidney-dialysis treatment was so scarce and expensive a secret committee was formed to decide which patients got treatment—and which died.

As was true then, McGough says, these super-expensive new drugs "are pushing at the question of limited resources." Decisions can't simply be left to insurers and employers, he said, because they require a broad social policy about what's "sustainable, ethical and equitable."

Group Health's Carlson says he reluctantly ponders price controls. "Is 'The sky's the limit' a tolerable national policy?"

Getting Help with Costs

Many programs exist to help patients with expensive medications, but patients often say they're difficult to negotiate.

Sally Garcia, the MS patient, has struggled to pay for Copaxone, "the only drug that worked for me," for five years.

Off and on, she's received help, but never for long. Last year, she dashed off an anguished letter to government agencies and every politician she could find.

"I ask you, 'How could the wealthiest nation in the world allow their disabled to go without medications specifically designed to promote their quality of life?'" she beseeched them.

For three months, she got help from the National MS Society's local chapter, and she switched plans.

Then, out of the blue, she began getting aid from an organization she says she's never heard of and never contacted.

She's grateful, but she worries the help will vanish as mysteriously as it arrived.

"This is going to go on until the day I die," she predicts. "I'll be this 90-year-old lady fighting for her Copaxone."

| "The average price of a generic is about $20 versus a comparable brand at around $120."

Generic Drugs Reduce the Cost of Prescriptions

Lori Chordas

In the following viewpoint, Lori Chordas claims that generic versions of prescription drugs significantly cut medication costs. Generics save consumers up to $10 billion at retail pharmacies each year, and switching from brand-name drugs can cost between 30 to 80 percent less, asserts Chordas. Insurers that promote generics, she adds, save their members millions of dollars in copayments, keep premiums from increasing, and—when medications are used as prescribed—reduce the likelihood of hospitalization or emergency care. And with patents expiring on expensive medications, she notes, many will go generic in the near future. Chordas is senior associate editor of Best's Review, *a magazine covering the insurance industry.*

As you read, consider the following questions:

1. In the author's words, why are generics safe and effective?

Lori Chordas, "Refilling a Need: Thanks to a Growing Number of Generic Drugs, Health Plans Are Better Able to Manage Prescription Costs," *Best's Review*, vol. 109, no. 4, August 2008. Copyright © A.M. Best Company, Inc. Reproduced with permission.

2. Why are generics lower in price, according to Chordas?

3. According to the author, what do experts anticipate about biologic drugs and generics?

When Leviton Manufacturing Co. Inc., a North American producer of electrical and electronic products, wanted to provide its employees some refuge from rising health care costs, it promoted the use of generic drug alternatives.

One of the most recent efforts includes participation in Blue Cross and Blue Shield of North Carolina's Medication Dedication program, in which copays are waived on all generics that treat congestive heart failure, high blood pressure, high cholesterol and Type 2 diabetes.

Now, Leviton is seeing a more than 60% generic utilization rate among its 3,500 employees, which exceeds the national average.

That generates into significant cost savings for both employees and the company, said Fran Ruderman, senior director of benefits and compensation.

Savings are becoming more widely recognized. In 2007, commercially insured Americans and benefit plan sponsors saw nearly a $5.2 billion savings in prescription drug costs thanks to greater use of generic drugs, according to pharmacy benefit manager [PBM] Express Scripts.

That year, the average cost of a prescription increased by only $1.09, to $54.34. Without what Express Scripts calls the "generic effect," the cost per prescription would have increased $3.58, to $56.83.

In 2007, generic drugs accounted for 65% of prescription drugs dispensed, according to pharmaceutical market intelligence company IMS Health.

More Brands Will Soon Become Generics

Today, a host of brand-name medications along with many blockbuster drugs sit in the pharmaceutical pipeline, ready to lose patent protection over the next couple of years.

Each year, generics save consumers an estimated $8 billion to $10 billion at retail pharmacies, and even more when hospitals use generics, according to the Congressional Budget Office.

That's good news as prescription drug use continues to climb. An Express Scripts study found the number of people with at least one prescription increased from 67% to 74% between 2000 and 2006.

That growth is taking a toll on the health care system. The fifth annual Milliman Medical Index said the cost of health care for the average U.S. family with employer-sponsored health coverage will increase more than 7% this year [2008] due in part to rising prescription drug prices.

While the average copay for preferred brand-name drugs increased by $4.52, to $19.18 between 2002 and 2007, according to Express Scripts, the average copay for generics increased by only 86 cents, to $7.57 during that time frame.

Generics also are having a big impact among seniors. A recent study by Wolters Kluwer Health Source, which provides market data and analytics for pharmaceutical and biopharmaceutical manufacturers, found that generic drugs now own 63% of the Medicare Part D market, up from 50% less than three years ago.

Safe and Effective Alternatives

But, are generics safe and effective alternatives? The FDA [Food and Drug Administration] definitely thinks so. Generics undergo a rigorous scientific review to ensure that they're high quality, safe and effective. Generic drug manufacturers must demonstrate that a generic has the same dosage form, strength, route of administration, conditions of use and bioequivalence (the drug delivers the same amount of its active ingredient in the same amount of time as the brand drug) as the approved brand-name counterparts.

Health plans are helping members make the switch.

"It begins with benefit design," said Jackie Kosecoff, chief executive officer of Prescription Solutions, a UnitedHealth Group-owned PBM. "Many encourage members to use generics. In 2008, many of our Medicare programs moved to a zero copay when members choose to purchase drugs through our preferred mail-service facility."

A recent survey by consulting, outsourcing and investment services provider Mercer found that most employers use tiered copayments for their prescription drug benefits. The most common arrangement is a three-tier structure with increasing copay amounts for generics, formulary brand names and non-formulary brand-name drugs.

Leviton's plan design follows a slightly different model. Employees pay a $10 copay for generics, $25 for preferred brand drugs, $50 for nonpreferred drugs, and has a fourth tier for specialty drugs that has a $100 maximum copayment.

As part of its aggressive Medication Dedication program, Blue Cross and Blue Shield of North Carolina not only waived copayment for generics but also moved more than 40 drugs to treat chronic diseases, such as Glyset and GlucaGen for diabetes, from tier 3 to tier 2.

The Blues plan also is working with its PBM Medco Health Solutions' clinical pharmacists to educate Blues providers about generics. "The targeted practices that had at least comparatively lower generic dispensing rates versus total book of business are visited, and this year so far we've seen a four-point improvement in the generic dispensing rate for those practices," said Brian Ellison, director of pharmacy administration.

The compilation of efforts is paying off. Today, North Carolina Blues' generic dispensing rate is hovering near 64%, he said. "If the average price of a generic is about $20 versus a comparable brand at around $120, anything you do to make members switch will save money on your total spend."

One of its Blues counterparts, Blue Cross and Blue Shield of Rhode Island, recently wrapped up its yearlong "OTC [over-the-counter] Options" pilot program in which more than 4,600 members received over-the-counter allergy drugs, such as loratadine—the generic form of Claritin—free of charge. Members saved nearly $260,000 in copays, and the plan had a prescription drug cost reduction of more than $250,000, compared with the previous year's costs.

The plan also is bringing providers into the loop. In 2005, it began installing MedVantx Sample Center units, an ATM-like machine that provides free generic medical samples, in participating physicians' offices.

In July [2008], Independence Blue Cross began waiving copays until the end of the year for 75 generic drugs for chronic conditions for its members and AmeriHealth of Pennsylvania subscribers. The Blues plan expects to waive about $12 million in copays. Earlier this year it began offering employers plans with zero copays for generics.

Employers also are becoming more generics-minded, said Kosecoff. "They're aware of the value proposition inherent with the use of these alternatives. For them, the decision is the extent to which they want to motivate that."

Savings in a Bottle

Are efforts paying off?

Regence's robust decision-support tools for physicians and patients have "moved the needle significantly," said spokesperson Angela Hult. Members' generic fill rate is 66.2%, well above the national average, and its nearly 8,000 employees have set the bar even higher with their 68.8% fill rate, she said.

"Each percentage point represents savings of up to $19 million. Since 2000, our 3 million members have saved themselves $530 million," she said. "That's $530 million in medication costs we didn't have to raise premium rates to cover."

Most Popular Generics

The ten most dispensed generic drugs in 2007 in the United States

Acetaminophen and Hydrocodone
Lisinopril
Levothyroxine
Amoxicillin
Metoprolol
Hydrochlorothiazide
Metformin
Azithromycin
Simvastatin
Atenolol

Source: Generic Pharmaceutical Assoc. (IMS National Prescription Audit, National Sales Perspective, Nov. 2007)

TAKEN FROM: Lori Chordas, "Refilling a Need: Thanks to a Growing Number of Generic Drugs, Health Plans Are Better Able to Manage Prescription Costs," *Best's Review*, August 2008.

Switching to generics often can cost anywhere from 30% to 80% less than brand-name treatments. That's because generic manufacturers don't have the investment costs of developers of new drugs, which are developed under patent protection.

To put savings in perspective, Tara Higgins, a clinical pharmacist with the Rhode Island Blues plan, said the cost of a 30-day supply of heartburn and acid reflux disease medication Nexium may average about $165. The generic alternative costs only about $30 per month.

"We try to promote generics in a way that members share in the economic gain along with the health plan," said Kosecoff. "Consumers share twice because we make the cost of drugs lower and generics help keep premiums from rising."

There's also long-term cost savings, said Ellison. "When you look at total medical spend, if someone is taking medications as prescribed, that means the likelihood of having a major event like a hospitalization or ER [emergency room] visit is greatly reduced for five years out."

Plans are feeling the effects. Cigna Pharmacy Management has innovative programs that empower individuals and physicians to take advantage of the cost savings of generics through appropriate and timely education, incentives and encouragement. "Through these programs, we have improved the use of generics by more than 20% over the past five years for both our clients and the individuals we serve, leading to one of the industry's leading generic dispensing rates," said clinical pharmacist Yi Zheng.

Today, Cigna's generic dispensing rate [GDR] for its book of business is approaching 67% and the rate for its Medicare Part D business is 70%, said Zheng. "This is significant as every 1% improvement in the GDR results is about a 1% reduction in overall pharmacy cost for the average employer."

"Generics are the largest single area of focus for our clients in terms of saving money, driving out waste and improving affordability of benefit without compromising health care," said Dr. Ed Weisbart, chief medical officer for Express Scripts. He said the company's generic fill rate tops 65%.

But he hopes that rate will soon exceed 80%. "Learned financial incentives such as copays, tiered structure and step therapy have gotten us to the 65% success rate, but the other 15% gap will require more than just incentives. They'll involve social norms. . . . We need to match up specific messages with predictable audience segments," he said.

"For instance, more than 30% of people who received letters from us about drugs going generic made the switch, but nearly 50% of our mail order customers who knew our brand choose the generic form. The difference? We had permission to talk to them."

Savings don't happen overnight, said Higgins. "For the first six months after a generic becomes available, due to generic exclusivity, the cost is still relatively high, usually about 10% to 15% off the branded drug. Costs then dramatically decrease."

Pharmacy Pipeline

There's more good news on the horizon.

A number of drugs that total billions of dollars in current drug spending could lose patent protection over the next five years. Some of the products expected to come off patent in 2008 include Sarafem for premenstrual dysphoric disorder, Depakote for seizures, Cipro HC for external ear infections, and Dovonex for psoriasis.

The following year, Prevacid for acid-related disorders is expected to go generic, said Weisbart. And the industry is anxiously awaiting the loss of patent protection of cholesterol-lowering agent Lipitor, Effexor XR for depressive and panic disorders, Cozaar for hypertension, and Flomax to reduce male urinary symptoms in 2010, he added.

Just What the Doctor Ordered

Is awareness of generics growing?

"Yes," said Ellison. "We take every opportunity to explain to members the value of generics. We're competing against direct-to-consumer drug ads, so we have to be consistent and unrelenting in our message to tell them generics are effective and save money."

That's working, he said. "More people are hearing the message and heeding it."

That's also important to help increase medication adherence, he said. A 2008 Kaiser Health Tracking Poll found that 23% of Americans didn't fill a prescription in the past year because of cost.

Providers also are making the switch, Ellison added. "That's where our e-prescribing initiatives come into play to make sure they have the tools and information at their fingertips at the prescribing moment to know what alternatives to prescribe."

Experts also are watching the potential for biologic drugs to someday enter the generic arena, which would offer significant savings to the industry. Biologics—drugs derived from living sources such as humans, animals or microorganisms and grown in specially engineered cells as opposed to drugs synthesized using chemical reactions in the lab—are revolutionizing the treatment of diseases such as cancer, arthritis and hemophilia. Worldwide sales of biologic medications rose 12.5% in 2007 to $75 billion, according to IMS Health.

But generics are only "one lever to address" rising health care costs, said Ellison. "If you can increase medication adherence by moving people to generics, you're going to start making an impact on chronic conditions. If people with chronic conditions aren't taking their medications, that could lead to possible major health events like a heart attack. If we can get them to move to generics and stay on them, then there's where we'll really start impacting overall costs."

Since pharmacy benefits comprise only about 15% to 20% of total health care costs, said Keith Kringle, vice president of finance for Health Net Pharmaceutical Services, "generics themselves can't totally compensate for all the inflation we see in other components of health care like hospitalization, physician and ancillary service costs. But it certainly can make a dent."

Periodical and Internet Sources Bibliography

The following articles have been selected to supplement the diverse views presented in this chapter.

Amy Allina	"The High Costs of Drug Costs," *Women's Health Activist Newsletter*, July/August 2007.
Dominic Coyle	"In Search of the Perfect Formula," *Irish Times*, October 29, 2010.
Michael Dickson and Jean-Paul Gagnon	"The Cost of New Drug Discovery and Development," *Discovery Medicine*, June 2009.
Katherine Eban	"Are Generic Drugs a Bad Bargain?," Today.com, May 26, 2009. www.today.com.
Economist	"Generic Drugs and Competition: Something Rotten," August 6, 2009.
Jim Edwards	"10 Reasons Drug Prices Always Go Up—and What We Can Do About It," BNET, March 15, 2011.
Kathleen A. Fairman	"The Future of Prescription Drug Cost-Sharing: Real Progress or Dropped Opportunity?," *Journal of Managed Care Pharmacy*, January/February 2008.
William Faloon and Saul Kent	"Slashing the High Cost of Prescription Drugs," *Life Extension Magazine*, April 2007.
Peter Keating	"Next Frontier in Health Care: Specialty Drugs," *SmartMoney*, May 4, 2009.
Multinational Monitor	"Eyes on the Prize: Incentivizing Drug Innovation Without Monopolies," May/June 2009.
Rebecca Ruiz	"What You Should Know About Generic Drugs," *Forbes*, July 27, 2009.

For Further Discussion

Chapter 1

1. Leslie Brody suggests that pharmaceutical trials offer promising experimental treatments to terminally ill volunteers. Carl Elliot, however, maintains that they merely promote drugs and place patients at serious risk. In your view, which author provides the more compelling argument? Use examples from the viewpoints to support your answer.

2. Marcia Angell contends that industry-sponsored clinical trials are inherently biased and designed to promote drug sales. In your opinion, does Caroline McGeough successfully counter Angell's claim in her argument that research organizations can control bias through regulation? Cite examples from the texts to support your response.

Chapter 2

1. Janet Woodcock explains that premarket testing may not detect all of a drug's problems. In your opinion, does this assertion undermine her position that the Food and Drug Administration (FDA) ensures the safety and effectiveness of drugs? Why or why not?

2. In your opinion, would Rebecca Burkholder's guidelines for administering behind-the-counter drugs protect consumers? Why or why not? Quote from Sidney M. Wolfe in your answer.

Chapter 3

1. John Patrick Oroho, Christine N. Bradshaw, and Christopher R. Corallo insist that pharmaceutical marketing is strictly regulated. Nonetheless, Susan Heavey and Lisa

Richwine write that the FDA is outgunned by drug advertising, especially in social media. In your opinion, which side makes the more persuasive argument? Use examples from the viewpoints to support your answer.

2. Steven P. Higgins argues that drug companies attempt to influence doctors with gifts. In your view, do any of the relationships defended by Bradley P. Knight fall under unethical practices? Cite examples from the texts to explain your response.

Chapter 4

1. PRWeb Newswire contends that prescription costs are so high in America that people are increasingly going online to order drugs from foreign pharmacies, such as in Canada, but can be duped by fraudulent operations. On the other hand, Charles L. Hooper maintains that drug companies price their products lower for many foreign buyers but deem Americans to be able to pay the higher prices—which helps pay the companies' costs. Do you think Americans should be allowed to continue buying prescription drugs online? Why or why not? How might these two authors answer this question?

2. Lori Chordas contends that generic drugs are lower in price than prescriptions because of the lack of development costs. Carol M. Ostrom argues that more drug companies are developing biopharmaceuticals, which cost much more than even brand-name drugs. In your opinion, should insurance cover these pricey drugs? Why or why not?

Organizations to Contact

The editors have compiled the following list of organizations concerned with the issues debated in this book. The descriptions are derived from materials provided by the organizations. All have publications or information available for interested readers. The list was compiled on the date of publication of the present volume; names, addresses, phone and fax numbers, and e-mail and Internet addresses may change. Be aware that many organizations take several weeks or longer to respond to inquiries, so allow as much time as possible.

American Medical Association (AMA)
515 N. State Street, Chicago, IL   60654
(800) 621-8335
website: www.ama-assn.org

The AMA is the largest professional association for medical doctors in the United States. It helps set standards for medical education and practices and is a powerful lobby in Washington for physicians' interests. The association publishes journals for many medical fields, including the monthly *Archives of Surgery* and the weekly *Journal of the American Medical Association* (*JAMA*).

Center for Drug Evaluation and Research (CDER)
Food and Drug Administration Division of Drug Information
Silver Spring, MD   20993-0002
(888) 463-6332
e-mail: druginfo@fda.hhs.gov
website: www.fda.gov/cder

CDER performs an essential public health task by making sure that safe and effective drugs are available to improve the health of people in the United States. As part of the Food and Drug Administration, CDER regulates over-the-counter and prescription drugs, including biological therapeutics and generic drugs. This work covers more than just medicines. For example, fluoride toothpaste, antiperspirants, dandruff shampoos, and sunscreens are all considered "drugs" and fall under CDER's purview.

The Heritage Foundation
214 Massachusetts Ave. NE, Washington, DC   20002-4999
(202) 546-4400
e-mail: info@heritage.org
website: www.heritage.org

The foundation is a conservative public policy research institute that advocates limited government and the free market system. It believes the private sector, not the government, should be relied upon to solve social problems. It publishes monographs, books, Webmemos, and background papers explaining its stance on health care and Medicare reform, prescription drug cost controls, and drug importation.

Institute of Medicine (IOM)
The Keck Center, 500 Fifth Street NW
Washington, DC   20001
(202) 334-2352 • fax: (202) 334-1412
e-mail: iomwww@nas.edu
website: www.iom.edu

The Institute of Medicine, a branch of the National Academies of Science, serves as an independent scientific adviser to policy makers, professionals, community leaders, and the public. It strives to provide information on biomedical science, medicine, and health that is unbiased and grounded in science. Its many reports on health care and prescription drugs are available on the website.

National Association of Boards of Pharmacy (NABP)
1600 Feehanville Drive, Mount Prospect, IL   60056
(847) 391-4406 • fax: (847) 391-4502

e-mail: custserv@nabp.net
website: www.nabp.net

NABP is a professional association that represents the state boards of pharmacy in all fifty states, eight Canadian provinces, and several foreign countries. It assists its members in the development and enforcement of uniform standards of care to help protect public health. It publishes the *NABP Newsletter*, state newsletters in thirty-two states, and the *National Pharmacy Compliance News*.

National Center for Policy Analysis (NCPA)
601 Pennsylvania Ave. NW, Suite 900, South Building
Washington, DC   20004
(202) 220-3082
website: www.ncpa.org

The NCPA is a nonprofit public policy research institute that aims to develop and promote alternatives to government regulation and control of health care. It prints several health care newsletters, numerous health care policy studies, and commentaries on prescription drugs. Its website includes a section on health care under which its studies, policy backgrounders, and analysis briefs can be found.

National Institutes of Health (NIH)
9000 Rockville Pike, Bethesda, MD   20892
(301) 496-4000
e-mail: nihinfo@od.nih.gov
website: www.nih.gov

Part of the US Department of Health and Human Services, the NIH includes the National Human Genome Research Institute and the National Cancer Institute, as well as many others. Its mission is to discover knowledge that will improve the nation's health. It does so by conducting and supporting research, training research investigators, and helping disseminate medical information. The NIH also publishes online fact sheets, brochures, and handbooks.

National Pharmaceutical Council (NPC)
1894 Preston White Drive, Reston, VA   20191
(703) 620-6390 • fax: (703) 476-0904
website: http://npcnow.org

Supported by more than twenty of the nation's major research-based pharmaceutical companies, NPC sponsors research and education projects aimed at demonstrating the appropriate use of medicines to improve health outcomes. It focuses on the use of evidence-based medicine to help patients make the best, most cost-effective health care decisions. Monographs on disease management, newsletters, and other publications geared to policy makers, health care providers, employers, and consumers are available on its website.

Pharmaceutical Research and Manufacturers of America (PhRMA)
1100 Fifteenth Street NW, Washington, DC   20005
(202) 835-3400 • fax: (202) 835-3434
website: www.phrma.org

PhRMA represents US drug research and biotechnology companies. It advocates public policies that encourage discovery of important medicines, and its medical officers sometimes testify before Congress on issues such as drug advertising, safety, and importation. It publishes newsletters, fact sheets, reports, and policy papers such as "Improving Prescription Medicine Adherence Is Key to Better Health Care."

World Health Organization (WHO)
Avenue Appia 20, Geneva 27   CH-1211
    Switzerland
e-mail: info@who.int
website: www.who.int

WHO has been operating its International Drug Monitoring Programme since 1968. It publishes the *World Health Report* annually and *WHO Drug Information* four times a year. Its website also includes information on the access, pricing, and policies relating to medicines and pharmaceuticals.

Bibliography of Books

Roberto Abadie *The Professional Guinea Pig: Big Pharma and the Risky World of Human Subjects.* Durham, NC: Duke University Press, 2010.

John Abramson *Overdosed America: The Broken Promise of American Medicine.* New York: HarperPerennial, 2008.

Ryan S. Blanton, ed. *Generic Drugs: Needs and Issues.* New York: Nova Science, 2009.

J. Douglas Bremner *Before You Take That Pill: Why the Drug Industry May Be Bad for Your Health.* New York: Avery, 2008.

Shannon Brownlee *Overtreated: Why Too Much Medicine Is Making Us Sicker and Poorer.* New York: Bloomsbury, 2007.

Mark Davison *Pharmaceutical Anti-counterfeiting: Combating the Real Danger from Fake Drugs.* Hoboken, NJ: Wiley, 2011.

Carl Elliot *White Coat, Black Hat: Adventures on the Dark Side of Medicine.* Boston: Beacon, 2010.

Lawrence T. Friedoff *New Drugs: An Insider's Guide to the FDA's New Drug Approval Process for Scientists, Investors, and Patients.* New York: PSPG, 2009.

Irving Kirsch *The Emperor's New Drugs: Exploding the Antidepressant Myth.* New York: Basic Books, 2010.

John L. LaMattina *Drug Truths: Dispelling the Myths About Pharma R&D*. Hoboken, NJ: Wiley, 2009.

Jacky Law *Big Pharma: Exposing the Global Healthcare Agenda*. New York: Basic Books, 2006.

Life Extension *FDA: Failure, Deception, Abuse: The Story of an Out-of-Control Government Agency and What It Means for Your Health*. Mount Jackson, VA: Praktikos Books, 2010.

Morton A. Meyers *Happy Accidents: Serendipity in Modern Medical Breakthroughs*. New York: Arcade, 2007.

Ray Moynihan and Allen Cassels *Selling Sickness: How the World's Biggest Pharmaceutical Companies Are Turning Us All into Patients*. New York: Nation Books, 2006.

Rick Ng *Drugs: From Discovery to Approval*. Hoboken, NJ: Wiley, 2009.

Clifford L. Nilsen *Generic Drugs: A Consumer's Self-Defense Guide*. Bloomington, IN: iUniverse, 2011.

Alex O'Meara *Chasing Medical Miracles: The Promise and Perils of Clinical Trials*. New York: Walker, 2009.

Melody Petersen   *Our Daily Meds: How the Pharmaceutical Companies Transformed Themselves into Slick Marketing Machines and Hooked the Nation on Prescription Drugs.* New York: Farrar, Straus & Giroux, 2008.

Adriana Petryna   *When Experiments Travel: Clinical Trials and the Global Search for Human Subjects.* Princeton, NJ: Princeton University Press, 2009.

Susan M. Reverby   *Examining Tuskegee: The Infamous Syphilis Study and Its Legacy.* Chapel Hill: University of North Carolina Press, 2009.

Peter Rost   *The Whistleblower: Confessions of a Healthcare Hitman.* Berkeley, CA: Soft Skull, 2006.

Robert L. Shook   *Miracle Medicines: Seven Lifesaving Drugs and the People Who Created Them.* New York: Portfolio, 2007.

Lorna Speid   *Clinical Trials: What Patients and Volunteers Need to Know.* New York: Oxford University Press, 2010.

John Virapen   *Side Effects: Death. Confessions of a Pharma-Insider.* College Station, TX: Virtualbookworm.com, 2010.

Martin A. Vout   *The Generic Challenge: Understanding Patents, FDA & Pharmaceutical Life-Cycle Management.* Boca Raton, FL: Brown Walker, 2008.

Index